You Can
Start
Your Own
Business

Jeffrey Davidson and Arnold Sanow

An "i can."™ Book
Business Series

Washington Publications, Inc.

Nags Head, N.C.

Published by
Washington Publications, Inc.
6810 Virginia Dare Trail
Nags Head, N.C. 27959

ISBN 0-925052-02-7
Library of Congress Catalog Card Number: 91-55308

A Word About "i can."™ Books

Welcome to WPI's "i can."™ books. This book is one in a series designed to help you achieve the success you deserve. The "i can."™ books cover a wide range of topics, from business and careers to relationships, health and literacy.

The "i can."™ books work from the idea that your attitude can be your best friend or worst enemy in helping you achieve what you want. Each book is based on the simple formula for success: the "i can."™ principle. This formula will help you assess your skills, talents and resources, then follow a pattern of time-tested steps which lead you to the achievement of your goals.

Like a map, each book shows you how to get to where you want to go, what it will take to get there, and how to steer around obstacles you will face along the way.

The "i can."™ books are easy to read, understandable and free of textbook drabness and jargon. The material is presented in a format which allows you to either read it cover to cover or use it for quick reference and reminders.

Throughout each book, you'll find highlighted quotes — easy to locate and immensely important advice from leaders in the field.

At the end of each book, you'll find a kit of important documents to get you started and a list of resources to help you further your understanding of the task at hand.

Finally, you will be guided through each book by Naci™ (pronounced knock-ee; "i can" spelled backwards). Naci™ is your guide on your journey to a better and more successful life. He is here to bring calm to chaos, to offer you solid support and the right mix of information. WPI is here to help you, too.

Ask about the book, *You Can Get There From Here,* which contains the "i can."™ formula, and other WPI publications. For more information, call 1-800-468-4226.

We wish you the greatest success. We are certain that the "i can."™ series will give you the knowledge and the confidence that comes with saying "i´ can."

Elizabeth F. Jones
Publisher

You Can
Start
Your Own
Business

"The business of America is business."
— Calvin Coolidge

Contents

Preface

From the time we are very small, most of us are continually told that we can't do certain things. This book, however, tells you that if you are willing to follow established guidelines and if you have the determination and energy, you *can* start your own business.

Beginning a business is a widely sought-after goal for those in the corporate world, retired people, or even for those who are new to the working world.

Being successful in your own business is a great equalizer for women or anyone in a socially or economically disadvantaged group.

This book is designed to start you thinking in the right direction. Use it, mark it up, and make your dream come alive.

We encourage you to write us, in care of WPI, with your stories and suggestions. Point your way to success with this book.

— Jeffrey P. Davidson and Arnold Sanow

Introduction

The opportunity to start your own business has never been greater than it is today. Worldwide markets are opening, and entrepreneurs of all descriptions are discovering that they can indeed be successful in their own ventures.

The decision to go into business for yourself must be a *business* decision, following months of planning, discussion and contemplation. It must not be based on impulse, whim or emotional fervor. It's an important, strategic life decision, one that will impact your family, your finances and your outlook on life.

We are enthusiastic about what this book can do for you, and we hope that you find it to be an important first step and valuable tool in guiding you to success.

We've found that most entrepreneurs are made, not born. So let's get started by discussing in Chapter One common traits that many successful entrepreneurs have, but let's also remember that determination can conquer all!

— Jeffrey Davidson and Arnold Sanow
February, 1991

The *Washington Post* has called **Jeffrey Davidson** "a human dynamo of business book writing." Jeff has written 11 hardcover books in four years. Of these, six have been translated into other languages, including Japanese and Chinese. Jeff is a certified managment consultant and a nationally known speaker on business and management topics. He is represented by Capital Speakers of Washington and Access Speakers of Little Rock, Ark.

• • •

Arnold Sanow, MBA, presents more than 130 lectures and serves about 100 clients annually. His clients range from start-up and growth-oriented companies to firms in trouble. Arnold provides marketing strategies, business and marketing plans, and management consulting. He also is a frequent guest on radio and television shows, and he recently hosted his own popular radio talk show in the Washington, D.C. area. He can be reached at 1-(800) 877-1972.

1

Do You Have What It Takes?

"Everything comes to him who hustles while he waits."

— *Thomas Alva Edison*

Chapter Chart

Do you want to succeed as a business owner, or entrepreneur? This chapter explains what an entrepreneur is and what kind of person finds success and fulfillment in starting his or her own business.

√ Webster's dictionary defines an entrepreneur as "one who organizes, manages and assumes the risks of a business or enterprise."

√ Research shows that successful entrepreneurs are upbeat, goal-oriented, comfortable with taking risks, organized, committed, energetic, adaptable, authoritative, responsible, self-aware and persevering.

√ Common weaknesses of entrepreneurs include poor judgment, permitting interruptions and working without a well thought-out plan.

√ You can test your business potential by taking the quiz at the end of the chapter. Your answers will help you judge whether you have the personality, skills and drive to be your own boss. Remember, if you think you can, you're right!

Do You Have What It Takes?

Introduction

Going into business for yourself remains one of the most exciting, fulfilling and challenging things you can ever do. It could also be one of the most risky and difficult. But if you are committed to making your business work and take into account the pitfalls that may lie ahead, you, too, can join the ranks of those who have turned their business dreams into reality.

Your Road Map To Success
"i can." ™

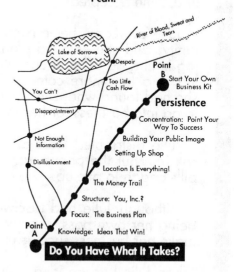

The Toughest Boss of All: A Success Story

Julie, a single mother and high school dropout with three children, receives some child support.

She worked as a chef's assistant in a neighborhood restaurant. She was responsible for planning the menus and supervising the staff in the chef's absence. Then the restaurant was sold and Julie was unemployed.

Aware of Julie's plight, a former customer asked if she'd like to cater a brunch the following weekend. Julie accepted.

Julie overcame her anxiety about the new opportunity, and she enjoyed planning, cooking and being in charge. The brunch went very well — and it led to a few more catering jobs. Julie soon knew she had found what she wanted to do. She decided to go into business for herself.

Julie distributed fliers and waited for the jobs to roll in. But the phone was depressingly silent and bills began to pile up.

Although Julie had discovered the satisfaction of being her own boss, she needed something more to make her business successful.

Then Julie had an idea. She remembered the customers who had appreciated her service. How could she get their business again?

What if she set up a catering service that delivered? She could cater private lunches and dinners for her old customers and business lunches for offices in the area.

She assembled a suitable crew of her former workmates. She contacted offices and residences in the neighborhood.

She did so well she amazed herself. In a few weeks, business was booming. Without a high school diploma or special training, Julie was now a successful business owner — her own boss, as well as the boss of others. And she had created a better life for herself and her family.

Prepare To Amaze Yourself

People like Julie, with little more than a good idea and a few friends to help, often amaze themselves. The energy that results from a focused, concentrated effort in making a successful business venture enables them to accomplish more than they ever did at a job.

Entrepreneurs are often the toughest bosses of all. The late night and weekend hours they dreaded when working for someone else become less work and more challenge.

How Do You Match Up?

In recent years, much attention has been paid to whether entrepreneurs are made or born. Research indicates that heredity, educational background, work values, family traits and environmental circumstances have a profound influence on an individual's decision to become a business owner. Since we have worked with over 225 business owners in more than 60 lines of work, we have come to know and appreciate the traits and values shared by successful entrepreneurs. Some of their common strengths appear below.

". . .If entrepreneurs are distinguished by anything, it is by the simple fact that they act on thoughts most everyone at one time or another has had."

— Thomas Jones
Entrepreneurism

Common Strengths of Entrepreneurs

Upbeat — Are positive and open to new possibilities.

Goal-Oriented — Have the ability to enlist others around them in pursuit of goals.

Reward-Seeking — Need to be visibly rewarded for their creativity and risk taking.

Comfortable with Risk — Thrive on a certain degree of risk.

Organized — Create systems that accomplish the task at hand.

Committed — Have a "whatever it takes" attitude.

Energetic — Have high energy and get sick far less often than normal.

Adaptable — Are able to modify their behavior to meet changing conditions.

Authoritative — Are self-assured and willing to take charge.

Believable — Appear to be genuine people.

Responsible — Recognize that they control their own destiny.

Self-Aware — Have an understanding of what they do well and what they don't do well.

Persevering — Are willing to keep going when most people would give up.

Each of the strengths shared by entrepreneurs can be taken to extremes to become a weakness. For example, the business owner committed to working hard may abandon the family and friends that serve as an essential part of his or her support system.

Or an excessively organized entrepreneur may waste valuable time fine-tuning procedures — time that could be better spent generating new business.

In addition, we've observed traits of many business owners which work against them. Such traits are listed on the page 9.

Paul Breaux, a real estate developer in North Carolina, put it this way . . .

I was very, very poor, and I had that drive, that focus on — I hate to say financial success, because as we all know now, success isn't measured in numbers of dollars. That has nothing to do with it. Money is a dissatisfier. If you have it, it won't make you happy. If you don't have it, then it can make you unhappy. So it is a negative as far as motivation. What I wanted to do was show myself that someone can come out of meager means — my father left my family when I was twelve years old, so I didn't have a lot of male influence in my life. I felt abandoned. I think that is perfectly normal. I felt like I had to come out of that — that I was better than the situation I had been left in. So I wanted to prove, not only to myself but to prove to all of my friends, that I was more than I appeared to be. I was more than cheap, ratty, little apartments, and hot dogs and beans. I was different than that.

That just happened to be the circumstance that I was in at the time.

The most important step in any journey is the first step. Make sure you are dedicated to seeing it through. Focus on the idea that you will be successful. Tell yourself that you will be successful and do all of those things which make you achieve your goals. That is the most important thing besides having drive. Know where you are going. Be a goal setter. Live by your goals — short term goals, and long term goals. But know where you are going, and don't take advantage of opportunities that don't lead you toward your goal. You could get side-tracked in business and opportunities in life, but if it is not leading you toward your goal, then get off it.

Test Your Business Potential

It's never easy to decide if starting your own business is a good idea. Few people know if they have the determination and skills necessary to be successful. Therefore, it's wise to test your motivations and desires before starting to organize a business.

The short questionnaire on page 10 will help you decide. It covers the main points in assessing business readiness. Read the questions and answer them truthfully. Your answers will reveal a great deal about your potential as an entrepreneur.

Common Weaknesses of Entrepreneurs

Establish unrealistic time frames — Seek to achieve challenging goals quickly, and often underestimate the time and resources that will be necessary to achieve them.

Attempt to accomplish too much alone — Do not sufficiently delegate authority, tasks or responsibilities to subordinates. Also, many maintain hidden agendas that they attempt to accomplish by themselves.

Tolerate interruptions — Leave themselves wide open to interruption. The biggest culprits here are the telephone and the unscheduled appointment.

Work without a plan — Prepare an extensive plan at the start of a business, and then toss it in a file and forget about it. They tend to have an impulsive management style which can lead them in circles.

Do not do enough homework — Proceed into untested waters without sufficiently researching the prevailing environment. This can be a fatal mistake. The more preparation made in the initial steps of any venture, the easier it is in the long run.

Test Your Business Potential

1. To do any task successfully, it is crucial to:

(a) do the job with as little wasted motion as possible.
(b) do the job slowly and with determination.
(c) find out all you can about the job before you begin.

2. In choosing a role model, you would select someone:

(a) of great determination and understanding.
(b) who can grasp power and who knows how to use it.
(c) who is in complete control of his or her own destiny.

3. To succeed at any undertaking, it is more important to:

(a) set a goal and stick to it no matter what happens.
(b) set a proper goal or objective at the beginning.
(c) shift ground quickly when you realize that you are losing.

4. In a critical situation that may be fatal, you try:

(a) to think up a brilliant idea that will free you from trouble.
(b) to improvise your way out of difficulty, one cautious step at a time.
(c) to stick to the commendable and decent way of doing things.

5. You're proud of your work history, which includes:

(a) important jobs in large, successful firms.
(b) a series of short-lived jobs which have moved you slowly upward.
(c) being fired from important jobs more than once.

6. Your choice for the best assistant is always a person who is:

(a) dull, but honest and uncompromising.
(b) brilliant, conceited, self-centered, but non-competitive.
(c) talented, imaginative and intelligent.

7. **In working day-to-day, you:**

  (a) dislike working for people who
      are foolish and boring.
  (b) dislike working for people who
      don't know what they are doing.
  (c) dislike working for anybody.

8. **If you are entrusted to execute a
dangerous mission, the first thing to do
is:**

  (a) make sure your course of action
      is foolproof.
  (b) proceed with caution, determi-
      nation and intelligence.
  (c) take as many calculated risks as
      possible.

9. **When you gamble, you always bet:**

  (a) on a sure thing.
  (b) across the board.
  (c) on a long shot.

10. **In a complicated business situation
that demands the proper approach, you
would rather:**

  (a) work with a colleague who has
      already shown talent, is re-
      sourceful and trustworthy.

    (b) work with a business partner or colleague who is a good friend and can be trusted.
    (c) work with an expert who is also a total stranger.

11. To ensure effectiveness in any act, it is neccessary to make certain that:

    (a) everything is satisfactory in every detail.
    (b) each performance is an improvement over the last.
    (c) each performance is as good as it can be.

12. To reach a certain destination, you can choose one of three trails. Your choice would be:

    (a) the winding trail that encounters beautiful, peaceful countryside.
    (b) the shortest, quickest and simplest trail to the destination.
    (c) the slippery trail that encounters dangerous rocks, landslides and other perils to the eventual goal.

Scoring Your Answers

1. The answer is (C). The best way to do any task is to understand what the task requires and meet those requirements. Although efficiency and determination seem like effective methods of achieving goals, finding out what the situation calls for
   is always the best way to reach a successful conclusion.

2. The answer is (C). To be in control of one's own destiny is the
   crucial element in starting a business. Although choosing a
   role model who is determined and powerful is important and
   noteworthy, these qualities are usually secondary to being in
   control of what lies ahead.

3. The answer is (A). Sticking to your goal, no matter what obstacles you face, is important since these obstacles will provide
   you with many reasons to give up over time.

4. The answer is (B). The entrepreneur's basic way of doing
   things is improvising. The business owner goes for the bottom
   line, or getting results.

5. The answer is (C), although it seems it would be the worst possible answer. People who start their own businesses and succeed are strong-willed and fiercely independent, which may
   explain why they likely have been fired from jobs. They often
   hate to be supervised.

6. The answer is (B). A good second-in-command is someone
   who has the knowledge and talents you need, but not someone
   who wants to be commander-in-chief.

7. The answer is (C). Business owners succeed at what they do
   basically because they hate working for anyone but themselves.

8. The answer is (C). Starting a business, no matter how cautious
   you are, always involves risk. Although to succeed you must
   proceed with caution, determination, and intelligence, these

are only secondary considerations. And no plan is foolproof, except, of course, proceeding as if no plan is foolproof.

9. The answer is (**A**). Even though entrepreneurs are risk takers, betting on a long shot is far too risky, even if the winnings would be substantial. Also, betting across the board would consume too many initial resources, and the winnings would not be good enough. The business owner finds the sure thing and bets on that.

10. The answer is (**C**). The entrepreneur works with many types of people and is not concerned with whom he works — as long as he or she is an expert. Colleagues and friends can become sloppy or careless and may let you down.

11. If your work is satisfactory (A), you won't make it — your work must be excellent. If your performance is as good as it can be, it can always be better. The successful business owner continually outdoes himself (**B**). He is successful precisely because he always learns from past accomplishments and resolves constantly to do better.

12. A business owner is goal-oriented. Once a goal is defined, the only objective is to reach that goal by the simplest, shortest and quickest means possible (**B**).

Do You Have What It Takes?

If you scored eight or more of these questions correctly, chances are that you have the personality, skills and drive that you'll need to build a successful business. But since perseverance is probably the single most necessary quality shared by all successful entrepreneurs, understand that a lesser score means you should pay closer attention to the details and helpful suggestions offered in this book.

If you're committed to starting a business and believe you have what it takes to work for the toughest boss of all — *you* — then read on. In Chapter Two, we take up the topic of finding and developing your business idea.

Your Road Map To Success
"i can." ™

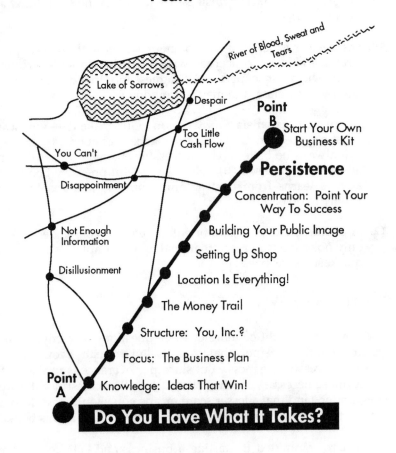

River of Blood, Sweat and Tears

Lake of Sorrows

Despair

Point B Start Your Own Business Kit

Too Little Cash Flow

You Can't

Persistence

Disappointment

Concentration: Point Your Way To Success

Building Your Public Image

Not Enough Information

Setting Up Shop

Location Is Everything!

Disillusionment

The Money Trail

Structure: You, Inc.?

Focus: The Business Plan

Point A

Knowledge: Ideas That Win!

Do You Have What It Takes?

Chapter Checkpoint

1. This chapter presented 13 common strengths that help make entrepreneurs successful. List them. Think about your own personality and skills and how they match up to the ones presented here. BE HONEST WITH YOURSELF!

   _____   _____

   _____   _____

   _____   _____

   _____   _____

   _____   _____

   _____   _____

   _____

2. Do you possess any of the common weaknesses entrepreneurs often have? Again, compare your own work habits and attitudes to the ones described. A large part of being successful in anything is anticipating weaknesses and overcoming them.

   _____

   _____

_____

_____

_____

_____

_____

3. What was the most surprising thing you learned
    in the Test Your Business Potential quiz?

_____

_____

_____

_____

Notes

Notes

2

Ideas
That
Win!

"No army can withstand an idea whose time has come."

— *Victor Hugo*

Chapter Chart

Does your business idea really have the potential to succeed? This chapter explains how to tell whether your idea will be a hit or a flop in the fickle world of business ownership. It also shows you how to turn losing ideas into winners.

√ **Opportunity is the watchword for would-be business owners. Have you found a need in the community from which you can profit?**

√ **Market research is the magic of wizards on Madison Avenue. Learn their secrets and reap the rewards of success!**

√ **If there isn't a need for your product or service, you may be able to create one with clever marketing techniques.**

√ **Competition can drive the best entrepreneurs underground. Learn how to make your product or service stand out from the crowd so that customers can't help but notice.**

Ideas That Win!

Introduction

The number one reason why you should start your own business amounts to one word: opportunity. If you see an opportunity to provide a product or service, generate enough money to cover your expenses and fatten your bankroll, then you're definitely on your way to business success.

Your Road Map To Success
"i can." ™

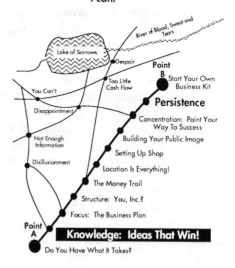

An Idea of Your Own

Where do you find opportunity? You can start by taking the time to think about your friends' and neighbors' lives. What is missing? What would make things easier, more pleasant and efficient for these people?

Some people set aside creative time — perhaps 15 minutes a day — for just such questioning, visualizing and dreaming. Indeed, many of the greatest people in history, from Moses to Mahatma Gandhi to Abraham Lincoln to Martin Luther King, have used time alone to sort things out, think things through or imagine a better way.

> **". . .Our best ideas — and business missions that are based on those ideas — most often spring out of our deepest personal motivations and interests."**
>
> **— Warren Avis**
> *Take a Chance to Be First*

Others, though, feel they can't set aside 15 minutes a day out of their overbooked lives. For these people, keeping an idea notebook is a viable option. Warren Avis, of Avis Rent-a-Car fame, suggests keeping a notebook handy at all times. "You never know when a great idea will strike," he says, "and you can't trust these things to memory alone."

From time to time go through your notebook and circle the best ideas, the ones that seem to jump off the page at you, the ones you love to dream about. Nurture these ideas. They are the golden seeds of your success.

Imagine a funnel — wide at the top, narrow at the bottom. It is through this kind of process you narrow down the number of ideas you have written in your notebook. Many ideas go in at the top and only a few come out at the bottom. The way to do this is simple.

A Funnel to Narrow Down the Number of Your Ideas

• First, the most important criterion for selecting your idea is personal preference. Select an idea that sparks your enthusiasm. This will help you commit your time, energy and money to making your idea work. Remember, if you are not excited, who else will be?

Enthusiasm for your business is essential — without it you will not succeed.

• Don't pick an idea merely because you think it is a safe investment or you've been told that it's profitable. There are no sure bets in business — and only your commitment, skills and imagination can transform your idea into reality.

• Take a look at the opportunities in your community to see if there is a need for what you'd like to do. If you want to sell fishing equipment, for example, but few people in your area fish, it's reasonable to assume your business will not flourish. Either change ideas or locales.

Match your idea with the needs of your community.

• Match your ideas with the needs of your target area through market research. Market research is what the wizards on Madison Avenue use to determine what consumers will buy and how much they will pay. You can use its magic, too, at little or no cost.

You probably have enough knowledge of your neighbors to make a few educated guesses about the kinds of businesses that would attract them.

If you live in a city, for example, you wouldn't set up a John Deere tractor dealership, would you? But you might be inclined to start a child care center, a gourmet take-out shop or a chic clothing

> "...Many hidden
> marketable needs are
> overlooked for years
> until someone spots
> those needs and sets
> out to fill them for cash.
> If there is a strong
> pent-up demand, the
> business explodes!"
>
> — Duane Newcomb
> *Fortune-Building
> Secrets of the Rich*

store. The difference is that the latter businesses offer products and services that city dwellers need and use: products and services that do some of their work for them, save them time or cater to their need to look professional and stylish.

The SBA can help you. Cost: FREE

• The Small Business Administration, a government agency charged with assisting small business owners to succeed, has conducted extensive research on the problem of matching small businesses with community needs and wants.

The agency lists six basic characteristics you should know about the people you intend to rely on for a customer base. Knowing these characteristics will point out the kinds of products and services that appeal to the people in your market area. Knowing more about your customers will help you judge the viability of your business idea.

**What Every Entrepreneur
Should Know about
Potential Customers**

• **General Characteristics**: age, sex, family type.

• **Social Characteristics**: education level, ethnic group, religion, leisure interests.

• **Labor Force Characteristics**: type of work, hours worked per week, number of wage-earners per family.

• **Income Characteristics**: sources and amounts of income.

• **Housing Characteristics I**: numbers of people per household, relationships of occupants, occupancy rate of housing in the area.

• **Housing Characteristics II**: rental versus ownership, size of housing per person.

SCORE has experienced assistance.
Cost: FREE

- Members of SCORE, the Service Corps of Retired Executives, are an experienced group of men and women who advise small business owners free of charge. When you go to a SCORE office, you will be assigned to a counselor who has worked in an industry or business related to your inquiry. SCORE is a program of the SBA.

The Census Bureau can help too!
Cost: Minimal

- You can find much information about your potential market in a book published by the U.S. Chamber of Commerce and the U.S. Bureau of the Census. *The Census Bureau of Population and Housing Report* presents data for almost every region in the country broken down into the categories listed on the next page.

    The book has an index in the front that allows you quick, easy access to the average characteristic in each category.

Census Bureau Categories

**Age by Sex
Persons per Household
Nationality
Educational Attainment
Occupation
Family (Household) Income
Number of Homes Owned
Number of Homes Rented
Number of People per Household
Value of Housing
Size of Housing**

The Commerce Department can help you too!
Cost: Minimal

• You can also find an overview of these facts in *The Urban Atlas Tract Data for SMSA*, published by the U.S. Department of Commerce.

Do your own research.
Cost: Minimal

• Conduct your own research to complete the general customer profile you've constructed. One way is to drive around the neighborhood where your potential customers live. You can see for yourself the number of cars in driveways, the size and condition of the housing, the presence or absence of children's toys and overall feeling of wealth or poverty in the area.

Testing the marketplace.
Cost: FREE

• Canvass the neighborhood. Talk to people about their needs and wants and the kinds of products and services they would use. To

Ideas   Ideas   Ideas   Ideas

Does Your Idea Spark Your Enthusiasm?
• • •
Is It an Opportunity in Your Community?
• • •
Does It Match the Needs of Your Target Area?
• • •
Do-It-Yourself Market Research:
SBA • SCORE • Census Bureau Commerce Dept.
• • •
Test the Marketplace
• • •
Consult the Experts

help with your survey, a list of questions for potential customers appears on the following page.

Consult the experts.
Cost: FREE

* Consulting experts in your community is an important component of your market research. People to contact include:
    teachers
    instructors or professors
    accountants
    experienced business owners
    business executives
    anyone else whose experience and knowledge leads you to believe they would be a useful source of advice about what the community needs and wants.

Sample Market Survey Questions

1. Do they currently buy products or services similar to the one you want to provide?

2. What do they like about what they're buying now? What do they dislike?

3. Can customers currently buy the product or service in their community? If not, would they like to? Have they ever been able to buy it in the community? If so, what happened?

4. At what time of the day can they buy the product or service? Is this satisfactory?

5. How many times and how often do they use the product or service? Would they use it more often if changes were made? What changes?

6. Are there any other products or services they would use if they were available in the community?

It sounds like a lot of work. *It is a lot of work.* But with so much money and time at stake, you need as much information and advice as possible before you start your business.

The business world, sadly, is full of people who had an idea that couldn't miss, but it did. Be armed with the right kind of information so your business story can end in success!

Create a Need!

Good market research can take you further than identifying a community's wants and needs. It can help you *create* needs.

> **When personal computers first came out, did you need one? Probably not. But now that your typewriter is gathering dust in the attic, you may think differently. Smart business people create needs that only they can fill.**

Identify Your Mission

Warren Avis of Avis Rent-A-Car believes you need to identify your mission. If you want to open a retail computer store, for example, then your mission is to sell a certain kind of computer (Apple? IBM? clone?) for a certain kind of customer (business? personal users?) in a certain kind of environment (full service retail? budget retail? wholesale? mail order?).

Marty Kingman, of Computers and Such in Fort Worth, Texas, decided that the "extra something" for his business would be training seminars, house calls to help customers set up their equipment, and a 24-hour telephone hotline for emergency questions. Because Kingman knew his customers' needs and wants, this simple idea enriched his business. This helpful idea added up to success!

The Extra Something

Your mission also includes supporting principles or factors which make your idea stand out from the competition. In the retail computer store, the supporting principle is this: To succeed, the store must give customers something the other stores don't.

Ideas   Ideas   Ideas   Ideas

Does Your Idea Spark Your Enthusiasm?
• • •
Is It an Opportunity in Your
Community?
• • •
Does It Match the Needs of
Your Target Area?
• • •
Do-It-Yourself Market Research:
SBA • SCORE • Census Bureau
Commerce Dept.
• • •
Test the Marketplace
• • •
Consult the Experts
• • •
Form Specific Objectives:
Mission
and Goals
• • •
Look at Your
Competition
• • •
Is It a Growth
Industry?

Outwit Your Competition

Your idea doesn't have to be completely original. In fact, originality can do more harm than good because you'll have to spend time and energy educating your potential market on what your product or service is and why they need it.

It is far easier to latch onto a familiar idea and find a way to improve it so it fills existing needs in a better and different way. By changing things a little, you can transform a good idea into an irresistible one.

Look at your competitors. Which aspects of their product or service are being handled poorly? Which aspects are being ignored? The answers spell opportunity for you.

Upgrading

One way to improve an idea is upgrading. In upgrading, you take a basic product and make it special by adding value or marketing it as a luxury item.

Designer blue jeans and gourmet cookies are basically the same as their more pedestrian counterparts. It's their marketing that makes them special.

People Express Airlines eliminated all of the extras that traditionally came with an airline ticket and caught hold of a budget market in the process.

Downgrading

This is the opposite of upgrading. To downgrade, you strip a product of its frills and offer it at a reduced price.

Good-Old-Days Feature

Another winning competition strategy is to bring back an old idea. Wouldn't it be wonderful if doctors started making house calls again? There may be a similar good-old-days feature that you can inject into your version of an existing product or service.

Bundling

Bundling is another way to improve on an existing idea. Bundling means putting two or more products or services together and selling them as a package.

Stereos were once sold only by component. Then some savvy business people bundled them. They put a radio, record player, tape player and speakers in one unit. These units are still selling today to customers who don't know a woofer from a capstan.

Unbundle It

Of course, if your competition is selling bundled products, you can always unbundle them and sell each piece separately. Tout the fact that customers can put together their own grouping just the way they like it.

Growth Industries

After shaping your idea to fit your community and your competition, you need to project it into the future to see how the passage of time, social trends and the development of new technology will affect it.

Some business ideas that were money-makers a few years ago are now money-losers. Drive-in movie theaters, for example, fell victim to the gas crunch, the subcompact car and the VCR. Make sure your idea is timely.

Some business ideas flourish as new technology becomes available. The VCR spawned a new industry — video-rental clubs — because someone realized that VCRs would take off as a consumer item and would support other businesses. The home entertainment industry is considered to have strong growth potential well into the next century.

Although you shouldn't limit yourself to so-called growth industries, your chances of success will be greater if you can read the industry signs and heed them.

```
Ten Best Business Bets
For The 1990s

Accounting and Auditing
Beauty and Personal Care Services
Computer Consulting
Conference Production and Planning
Child Care and Elder Care Services
Health and Fitness Clubs and Courses
Housecleaning and Errand Services
Real Estate Assistance Services
Temporary Employment Agencies
Travel Planning and Tour Organizing
```

The Longest Journey . . .
The Development of Your Idea

You have an idea. It has passed through the funnel of questions and qualifications. You've examined a potential market and you've found that a specific neighborhood, community or other market is one in which your business can succeed.

Now is the time to go into action. First, you need a plan. You may need start-up capital — yours or funding from others.

The best way to begin is to write a detailed, well-thought-out business plan. Chapter Three shows you the way to write your business plan.

Get ready to map your road to success!

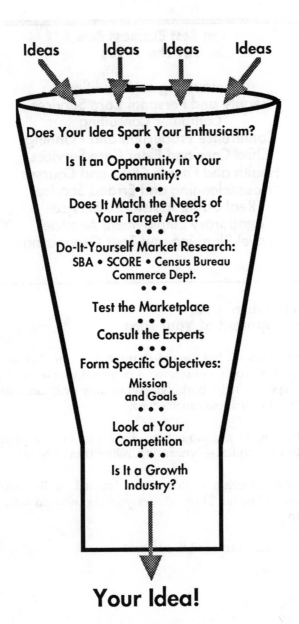

Ideas   Ideas   Ideas   Ideas

Does Your Idea Spark Your Enthusiasm?
• • •
Is It an Opportunity in Your
Community?
• • •
Does It Match the Needs of
Your Target Area?
• • •
Do-It-Yourself Market Research:
SBA • SCORE • Census Bureau
Commerce Dept.
• • •
Test the Marketplace
• • •
Consult the Experts
• • •
Form Specific Objectives:
Mission
and Goals
• • •
Look at Your
Competition
• • •
Is It a Growth
Industry?

Your Idea!

Your Road Map To Success
"i can." ™

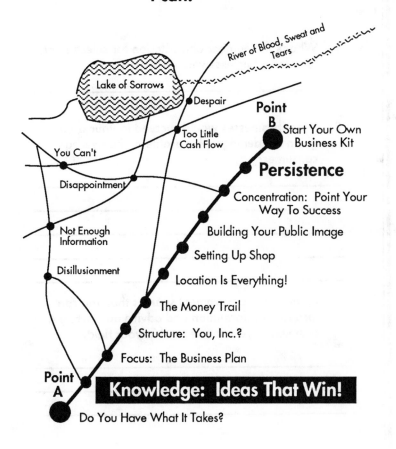

Chapter Checkpoint

1. What's the number one criterion for selecting an idea for a business venture?

   _____

2. What businesses would succeed in your area, given the demographic profile of the average consumer?

   _____

   _____

   _____

   _____

3. Name three government sources that you can turn to for information and advice on starting a business in your locale, and in your field.

   _____

   _____

   _____

4. Which of the eight competition strategies outlined in this chapter apply to your product or
   service?

   _____   _____

   _____   _____

   _____   _____

   _____   _____

5. What are some trends that will have an impact
   on your business in the next five years?

   _____

   _____

   _____

   _____

   Ten years?

   _____

   _____

   _____

   How will these trends affect your business?

   _____

   _____

   _____

   _____

Notes

3

The Business Plan: Mapping Your Road To Success

"Political skill: The ability to foretell what is going to happen tomorrow, next week, next month and next year. And the ability afterward to explain why it didn't happen."

— *Winston Churchill*

Chapter Chart

A business plan is a necessary tool for developing almost any business idea. This chapter explains how to write a business plan that will yield results for you.

√   The major components of the business plan are the executive summary, the goals section, the operations section and the financials. Each takes up a specific aspect of your business life.

√   It's important to work on your goals until they are clear. Fuzzy goals make it difficult to tell whether you and your employees can meet them.

√   You don't have to be a genius to work up the financial section of your plan. A few brief tables are all you need to show the financial picture of your idea.

The Business Plan: Mapping Your Road To Success

Introduction

You have your idea. You've done a lot of thinking about what you can do for your business and what it can do for you. You also have a fair understanding of who your business will serve and how you will make your product or service appealing.

Your next task is to focus on how you are going to make your business idea into a successful venture.

Your Road Map To Success
"i can." ™

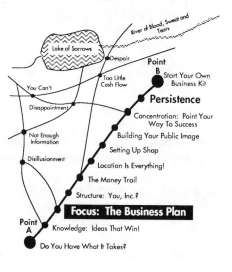

River of Blood, Sweat and Tears

Lake of Sorrows

Despair

Point B — Start Your Own Business Kit

Too Little Cash Flow

You Can't

Disappointment

Persistence

Concentration: Point Your Way To Success

Building Your Public Image

Not Enough Information

Setting Up Shop

Disillusionment

Location Is Everything!

The Money Trail

Structure: You, Inc.?

Focus: The Business Plan

Point A

Knowledge: Ideas That Win!

Do You Have What It Takes?

Take Time to Save Time

Most budding entrepreneurs like to skip a detailed planning phase. But, like it or not, it is an essential part of most successful businesses.

Business plans are neat little documents that organize all of the brainstorming you did in Chapter Two into a comprehensive statement about what you plan to do and how you plan to do it. They can prove that you are not only innovative, but realistic enough to verse yourself in the dynamic world of supply and demand, asset and liability, income and expense.

> " . . . A man's or woman's mind works in a peculiar way. Start it without direction and it operates in a purposeless, haphazard fashion. Give it a goal, however, and it will, like a computer, begin to take you in that direction."
>
> — Duane Newcomb
> *Fortune-Building Secrets of the Rich*

Writing a business plan has many benefits:

- It helps you focus on your idea, collect your thoughts and organize them in a logical, winning manner.

- It is a persuasive tool in convincing your family, friends, associates, and potential funding agents that you are committed to being an entrepreneur with a winning idea.

- It proves that you are not only innovative, but also realistic.

- It gives the particulars of how you will use the money passing through your checking account each month. This information is invaluable to you and your banker because a business that doesn't control its cash flow is a short-lived business.

- It serves as a road map through the development of your business and will help you focus on achieving success.

Many entrepreneurs think they don't have to plan because they just know what to do. Don't let such self-important talk fool you.

Some may not write a plan down and are able to juggle all of the vision's details in their heads.

For most people, however, the business plan is a practical storehouse of our most brilliant business ideas. It is our road map to success.

Even though it takes more than a little time for you to draw up your business plan, doing so will save you time and trouble in the long run. You won't have to deliberate on your options with three contractors on the line and a dozen impatient customers at your door. That only courts disaster.

For purposes of this chapter, we have identified each section of the business plan with a working title; for example, Section I: Goal Setting. When you write your business plan, however, you will want to title the goal-setting section with a more positive representation, such as "A One-Stop Shopper's Supermarket."

Anatomy of a Business Plan

While business plans are as varied as the businesses they describe, almost all include the same basic information about goals, operations and finances.

> # Title
>
> **Your name**
> **Your Business' name**
> **Address**
> **Telephone**
> **Date**

Anatomy of a Business Plan

- **Title Page**
  — Name of Document
  — Name and Address of Proposer

- **Executive Summary**
  — Brief Purpose of Business
  — Brief History of Company, Its Development,
    Products/Services and Marketing Strategy
  — Brief Explanation of Business Plan
  — Brief Summary of Financial Needs

- **Table of Contents**

- **Section I: Goal Setting**
  — One-Year Goals and Five-Year Goals:
    - Product Development
    - Market Development
    - Corporate Development
    - Financial Development

- **Section II: Business Development**
  — Basic Structure: Chart of Positions
  — Physical Resources

- **Section III: Operations**
  — Activities
  — Production Schedules
  — Personnel
  — Policies

- **Section IV: Financial Information**
  — Start-up Capital
  — Operation Budget
    1-year
    5-year
  — Balance Sheet

The First Page

The first page contains the name of the program. This identifies the name and address of the proposer, the date and any other information which is pertinent to the description of the business plan.

Executive Summary

In recent years planners have added a new section, the executive summary. This section introduces the firm and serves as an overview for the rest of the plan.

- It should be one page in length if possible; no more than two pages.
- It should answer some of the reader's questions while heightening interest in what is to follow.

- It briefly describes the purpose of your business. Think of it as the proverbial foot squeezing through the closing door — you want the shoe to look so good that the rest of you is invited in.

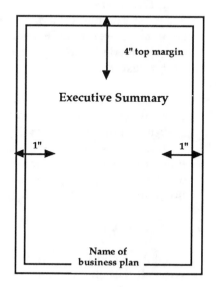

- The executive summary takes a broadstroke approach, presenting a brief history of your company, its development, its products and services, and its marketing strategy. The descriptions needn't include detailed facts and figures. They are treated in depth later in the plan.

Anatomy of a Business Plan

- **Title Page**
  — Name of Document
  — Name and Address of Proposer

- **Executive Summary**
  — Brief Purpose of Business
  — Brief History of Company, Its Development,
    Products/Services and Marketing Strategy
  — Brief Explanation of Business Plan
  — Brief Summary of Financial Needs

- **Table of Contents**

- It briefly describes the business plan itself: the information to be presented and the time periods covered by the plan — one year, five years, whatever is most suitable for your business. For most businesses, a one-year and a five-year plan are sufficient to set reasonable goals and, if needed, attract qualified investors.

- The summary presents the amount of money you are seeking. This helps busy investors know right away if they can help you before they've invested time to read the plan.

The Table of Contents

The table of contents is usually one page. It lists chapter numbers or titles and subsequent tables and documents.

Table of Contents

Executive Summary	1
Corporate Goals	3
Marketing Opportunities	5
Business Development	7
Exhibits	10

Name of
business plan

> • **Section I: Goal Setting**
> — **One-Year Goals and Five-Year Goals:**
>   - **Product Development**
>   - **Market Development**
>   - **Corporate Development**
>   - **Financial Development**

Section I: Goal-Setting

The goals section is the crux of your business plan. It takes the "what" of your business —what will be produced and/or offered — and projects it into the future. It is about possibility, vision and evolution. It is the section that inspires investors to believe in your dreams as much as you do. As a beginning entrepreneur you need two sets of goals: one-year goals and five-year goals. The one-year goals explain what you need to get started and your basic operation.

Saying "I want the business to turn a profit" is a worthwhile goal in itself, but it is far too vague to be useful. Better to state the goal in a way that makes it clear to everyone — you, your investors, and your employees — exactly what you are hoping to achieve in terms of profit. Something like "I want to clear $25,000 in net profits after one year of operation" gives you a concrete end result to work toward.

Next, your five-year goals list objectives which define your critical business path through its first five years.

Both sets of goals address the myriad aspects of doing business: products and services, marketing strategies, organization, resources, and more.

What follows is a list of topics you may want to cover in this section. You may need to add or delete areas for your business. Don't worry if you're not familiar with all the terms in the table. By the time you finish this chapter, they will have become second nature to you.

Subject Areas for Goal Setting

Area	One-Year Goals	Five-Year Goals
Product Development	Definition of products & services	Improvements to products & services New products & services
Market Development	Definition of market Market share & competition Marketing strategy	Expansion & specialization of market Gains in market share Changes in marketing strategy
Corporate Development	Basic structure of start up Basic resources of start up Operating policies & procedures	Growth of structure: lateral & vertical Expansion & upgrading of resources Changes to policies & procedures
Financial Development	Start up costs Operating budget of start up Volume of sales of start up Cost of goods sold of start up	Projected operating budget Projected volume of sales Projected cost of goods sold

Build Realistic Goals

As you establish your goals keep in mind:

- Goals have to be specific and easily measurable so you have a way of telling whether you've met them or not.

- Goals must be realistic. Goals that are set too high may lead to discouragement. Goals that are set too low may lessen motivation. Somewhere in between are goals which motivate you and your employees to work at a pace that's not too stressful and not too relaxed.

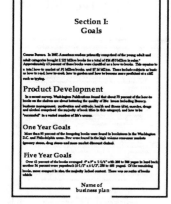

The Learning Tree Day Care Center in Houston, Texas, had as its opening goal providing supervision to a group of 10 one-year-olds to six-year-olds, Monday through Friday, 7 a.m. to 6 p.m., in a rented church basement in a residential neighborhood.

• • •

A messenger service in Philadelphia had a start-up goal of delivering 200 packages per week in the downtown area, by bicycle and on foot, during business hours.

• • •

In each case, the goal was modest and the limits of operation were set beforehand.

- Build realism into goals by breaking them down into smaller supporting goals called objectives — each with a time frame for completion.

For example

Your goal: 1,200 new subscriptions

Objective: 100 new names per month

Looking at the goal this way gives you the chance to quickly tell if you're on target — either you attained 100 new names or you didn't. If you didn't, find out why before you're hopelessly off track.

The Learning Tree decided to expand to 20 children and add a transportation service consisting of two rented vans with two minimum-wage workers during the first and last two hours of the operating day.

• • •

Fun on Wheels, a Hartford bicycle store, introduced a new line of all-terrain bikes and began giving seminars on basic repair.

Trouble-Shooting Your Goals

Successful business strategists prepare for disaster by presenting best case/worst case scenarios, working in extra time and alternate strategies for managing possible problems.

Sit down with someone outside of your business and ask: "What could possibly go wrong with this plan or procedure?" This way, you get input from someone not invested in making your dream work, someone who is free to be brutally honest about the flaws in your plan.

Product Development

One-Year Goals

If you're not operational yet, your product or service is an idea in your head. Your one-year goal, therefore, is to produce the product or service as you perceive it.

Five-Year Goals

In the five-year goals, you describe any modifications to the product or service, or any new products or services that you will implement once the one-year goal has been met.

Market Development

The goals section also presents your ideas on how you will make your marketing effort competitive.

One-Year Goals

Begin by describing the current market in great detail, contrasting the amount of business your competitors are doing (their market share) with the potential amount of business the market could support (the total market).

You also prove in this section that you know the market, including the basic psychology of your potential customers and what their basic needs are.

Are you going after the budget market? People in this market want products and services at low prices, with less emphasis on long-term quality or style.

Are you going for the luxury market? These people want products and services which allow them to feel pampered and support their image as people of good taste.

Once you've laid this groundwork, describe how you will reach this market and beat the competition.

Erika's Total Look, Inc., a full-service beauty salon in a Chicago suburb, emphasized that to attract upscale customers the ambiance of the salon would have to convey quality.

Erika outlined a detailed plan to install cathedral ceilings and skylights in the salon's interior and to have fresh-cut flowers at every station. The owner also planned to invest in a trendy advertising campaign to establish the salon's identity as an upper-crust establishment.

If you're going for the budget market, outline your plan for keeping production and delivery costs lower than those of your competitors, which will allow you to beat them on price. If you want to appeal to the luxury market, detail your plan for promoting the image of exclusivity of your product or service, or for adding elements to make it more attractive than your competitors' versions.

Five-Year Goals

After your initial goals have been outlined, project your marketing goals for the next five years. You might see your business adding staff or opening more stores in your area, thus grabbing a larger share of the local market. Or, you may wish to expand geographically, entering entirely new markets.

You may have an interest in a specialized market in your area which, while not your primary market, might be profitable. If so, outline your ideas on how and when you will go about reaching that secondary market.

Corporate Development

One-Year Goals

Include in your one-year goal description how you intend to structure your operation to make it work: the people, resources and procedures.

Five-Year Goals

For the five-year component of your corporate plan, project the expanded capabilities you will need to handle the expanded customer base you expect to be serving by then. You might need more equipment, upgraded machinery, or a more diversified plant as you branch out into new kinds of production and/or services.

Financial Development

One-Year Goals

This section contains a listing of projected start-up costs, the volume of anticipated sales, and the cost of goods sold. In the financial section, include an operating budget as described on page 59.

Five-Year Goals

Outline here what you will be doing five years from now, your vision of the volume of sales and projected cost of goods sold. You will want to attach a five-year projected operating budget in the financial section of your plan.

Say you're running a home-cleaning service. What happens when a lead comes in? Someone in your organization gets basic information from the caller, sets a fee, and arranges for an employee to be on the job at the specified time.

What happens when your employee arrives at the job site? Perhaps you have a certain cleaning regimen that you insist your employees use. Does the employee leave an invoice with the client or does your bookkeeper send one later?

Section II: Business Development

Once you've outlined your one-year and five-year goals describe how you will meet these goals.

In the business development section, describe the "how" of your operation. Prove to yourself and your investors that you have thought through how the different elements of business —people, resources and procedures — will come together to make your operation work.

Begin the section with a description of the basic structure of your start-up organization. The easiest way to do this is to make up a chart of the positions in your organization, with a descriptive paragraph for each position.

Next, describe the physical resources required for the operation of your business. For some, the equipment needed will be minimal. The messenger service in Philadelphia, for example, was started from the entrepreneur's home with two phone lines, two beepers, two bicycles and some supplies.

Other pursuits can be more equipment intensive. A laundromat business requires suitable space, washing machines, dryers, laundry carts, seats and a cash register.

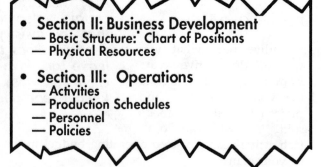

- • **Section II: Business Development**
  - — **Basic Structure: Chart of Positions**
  - — **Physical Resources**

- • **Section III: Operations**
  - — **Activities**
  - — **Production Schedules**
  - — **Personnel**
  - — **Policies**

Whatever your pursuit, think through your operation step-by-step and person-by-person. Don't be like one Dallas entrepreneur who forgot to get enough chairs for his staff to sit on!

One more word about resources. For many businesses, location might be the most valuable resource. See Chapter 6. Don't overlook this powerful aspect of building business success.

Section III: Operations

Activities

This section of your business plan describes exactly how you do what you do. It is a complete menu of your activities, starting with how you procure your raw materials through how you deliver finished goods to your customers.

Production Schedules

A heavyweight component of this section is the production schedules — what gets done at which step in the process and how much time it takes to do each step.

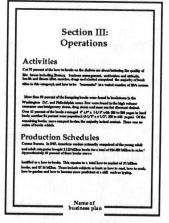

Personnel

Refer back to your section on structure, where you define the responsibilities of each position in your company. Now is the time to pull these positions together into a coherent process.

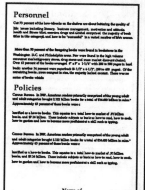

Though these details may seem obvious to you, it is important to spell them out in your plan. That way, when the leads start pouring in, you and your employees know what to do — without the hassle of the trial-and-error approach.

Policies

Mary's Learning Tree has a policy about children who are ill: If they have a fever, they must be taken home immediately. Knowing this, Mary's employees follow the procedure of calling parents immediately when a child's temperature exceeds 100° F.

Policies are an important part of this section. Policies are the rules that guide procedures.

In summary, your policies should be articulated clearly in your corporate plan. They will have a big impact on the procedures your employees follow.

Section IV: Financial Information

Finally, your business plan should address your financial picture over the next one-year and five-year periods. What kind of money do you need to start up? What does your budget look like? What are your realistic projections of revenues each year for the next five years? This part of the plan answers these and other questions about your company's financial situation.

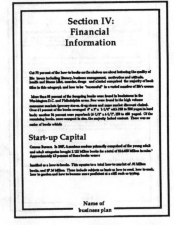

The basic elements of this section are the balance sheet, the operating budget and for beginning companies, the start-up-costs sheet.

The **balance sheet** is a picture of assets and liabilities. It shows your business' equity or net worth — how much you own versus how much you owe.

- **Section IV: Financial Information**
  — Start-up Capital
  — Operation Budget
    1-year
    5-year
  — Balance Sheet

The **operating budget** balances your income against your expenses. It gives you a periodic look at whether you are in the black or the red and by how much. For your first year of operation, you should report on the budget by the month. For subsequent years, an annual budget is enough.

Smith, Inc.
Projected Budget
January 1, 1991 through December 31, 1991

Projected Revenues		
Revenue	$ 101,388.96	
Interest Revenue	224.83	
Total Projected Revenue		$ 101,613.79
Projected Expenses		
Accounting and Legal	$ 2,301.27	
Advertising	6,240.00	
Bank Service Charges	83.19	
Contributions	1.00	
Dues and Subscriptions	4,068.66	
Editing and Layout	18,278.12	
Interest	2,198.40	
Insurance	1,668.34	
Leases	2,062.10	
Office	4,611.13	
Payroll	26,705.56	
Payroll Tax — Employer	2,161.27	
Petty Cash		
Postage	1,792.26	
Rent	11,520.83	
Repair and Maintenance	1,038.89	
Travel	2,482.44	
Entertainment	1,446.96	
	89.32	
	98.15	
	65.90	94,047.89

Smith, Inc.
Projected Budget
January 1, 1991 through December 31, 1995

	1991	1992	1993	1994	1995	Total for five years
Projected Revenues						
Revenue	$ 101,388.96	$ 101,388.96	$ 101,388.96	$ 101,388.96	$ 101,388.96	
Interest Revenue	224.83	224.83	224.83	224.83	224.83	
Total Projected Revenue	101,613.79	101,613.79	101,613.79	101,613.79	101,613.79	$ 508,068.95
Projected Expenses						
Accounting and Legal	$ 2,301.27	$ 2,301.27	$ 2,301.27	$ 2,301.27	$ 2,301.27	
Advertising	6,240.00	6,240.00	6,240.00	6,240.00	6,240.00	
Bank Service Charges	83.19	83.19	83.19	83.19	83.19	
Contributions	1.00	1.00	1.00	1.00	1.00	
Dues and Subscriptions	4,068.66	4,068.66	4,068.66	4,068.66	4,068.66	
Editing and Layout	18,278.12	18,278.12	18,278.12	18,278.12	18,278.12	
Interest	2,198.40	2,198.40	2,198.40	2,198.40	2,198.40	
Insurance	1,668.34	1,668.34	1,668.34	1,668.34	1,668.34	
Leases	2,062.10	2,062.10	2,062.10	2,062.10	2,062.10	
Office	4,611.13	4,611.13	4,611.13	4,611.13	4,611.13	
Payroll	26,705.56	26,705.56	26,705.56	26,705.56	26,705.56	
Payroll Tax — Employer	2,161.27	2,161.27	2,161.27	2,161.27	2,161.27	
Petty Cash						
Postage	1,792.26	1,792.26	1,792.26	1,792.26	1,792.26	
Rent	11,520.83	11,520.83	11,520.83	11,520.83	11,520.83	
Repair and Maintenance	1,038.89	1,038.89	1,038.89	1,038.89	1,038.89	
Travel	2,482.44	2,482.44	2,482.44	2,482.44	2,482.44	
Entertainment	1,446.96	1,446.96	1,446.96	1,446.96	1,446.96	
Taxes and Licenses	1,589.32	1,589.32	1,589.32	1,589.32	1,589.32	
Utilities	3,798.15	3,798.15	3,798.15	3,798.15	3,798.15	
Total Projected Expenses	94,047.89	94,047.89	94,047.89	94,047.89	94,047.89	$ 470,239.45
Projected Net Income	$7,565.90	$7,565.90	$7,565.90	$7,565.90	$7,565.90	$37,829.5

The **start-up chart** is a list of the expenses you will incur to put yourself in business and keep things going for a few months while sales pick up speed. It doesn't have to be anything fancy, and you only have to do it once in the life of your business!

This sounds like a lot of work, but keep in mind that much of the information in this section is repetitive. You're slicing the same pie several ways in an attempt to give your investors an understanding of how the whole pie works.

Startup Expenses Suzanne's Gourmet Take Out Target Start Date: June 15, 1987	
Leasing of Location	$ 10,000.
Renovation of Location	4,000.
Culinary Equipment	8,000.
Furniture	2,000.
Supplies	1,500.
Utilities	2,500.
Maintenance & Extermination	1,000.
Inventory	8,000.
Payroll (for two employees)	18,000.
Promotion & Advertising	1,500.
Legal & Accounting Services	4,500.
Licenses & Permits	3,000.
Insurance	1,000.
Taxes	4,000.
Interest	2,000.
Professional Membership	500.
TOTAL	$ 71,500.

If you like tinkering with things, doing jigsaw puzzles or juggling, you'll be a whiz at this section. However, if the word "mathematics" makes you want to run for the hills, take a deep breath and hold on: We'll make this as painless as possible. If you're still hopelessly befuddled after reading this section, forget the hills, and run for a sympathetic accountant. No sense creating a stumbling block for yourself — your business is too important!

The Balancing Act

The balance sheet is a statement of your financial situation at a particular point in time. It's referred to as a "balance" sheet because the number at the bottom of one section must be equal to the number at the bottom of the other. The balance sheet uses the basic equation of accounting:

$$\text{Assets - Liabilities = Equity}$$

Balance Sheet, December 31, 1991
Terry's Taco House

Assets
Current:

Cash in bank	$2,800.00	
Accounts Receivable	1,100.00	
Merchandise Inventory	3,000.00	
Prepaid Expenses	400.00	
Total Current Assets		$7,300.00

Fixed:

Store fixtures	1,500.00	
(less depriciation)	(25.00)	
Showcases	400.00	
Total Fixed Assets		$1,875.00
Total Assets		**$9,175.00**

Liabilities

Accounts Payable	$1,925.00	
Contract Payable	300.00	
Total Liabilities		**$2,225.00**
Equity (or Net Worth)		**$6,950.00**
Total Liabilities + Equity		**$9,175.00**

Assets are anything your business owns outright — perhaps its location, inventory or other goods.

Liabilities are the debts of your firm. When you subtract the dollar value of what you owe from the dollar value of what you own you get your business's actual cash value, referred to as **equity**.

Accountants, being a mysterious breed, use the equation in a slightly different form:

$$Assets = Liabilities + Equity$$

But don't let this equation fool you. It still means the same thing.

Shoestrings and Other Budgets

There are different kinds of budgets used to estimate income and expense activity in a business including a finished goods budget, cash budget and selling and general and administrative expense budget.

An operating budget provides a summary of income and expense projections of the different budgets as well as gross profit and net income projections. Budgets can range from a mere six lines to a hefty 60 pages long. Somewhere in between is the right length for you. Your budget should be as brief as possible, giving just enough information to be useful to potential investors.

Let's go through a fairly basic operating budget line by line. This one is for Bikes for Tikes, Inc., a children's outdoor toy store in Phoenix, Arizona.

1. **Estimate your sales.** Sales is the money you expect to receive for products or services sold during the period under review, taking into account any projected returns or cancellations.

2. **Estimate your cost of goods sold.** Cost of goods sold is an accountant's way of grouping together the expenses that you expect to incur as a direct result of producing the goods and services that you sell, including the costs of stocking and purchasing inventory and all labor costs involved with producing or handling products.

3. **Figure your estimated gross profit.** Subtract cost of goods sold from sales.

Bikes for Tikes, Inc.
Operating Budget
for the Year Ending December 31, 1991

Sales		$100,000.00
Cost of Goods Sold		
Model 1: 500 Units x $40.00 = $20,000		
Model 2: 400 Units x $80.00 = $32,000		
		52,000.00
Gross Profit		48,000.00
Selling and General and Administrative Expense		
Depreciation	2,000.00	
Advertising	1,000.00	
Salaries	23,000.00	
Insurance	5,000.00	
Utilities	1,000.00	
Interest	1,000.00	
		33,000.00
Income before Taxes		15,000.00

4. **Estimate your selling and general and administrative expenses.**
   These expenses include items such as supplies, rent and utilities,
   salaries, and other amounts you must pay just to stay in business,
   whether or not you produce or sell anything.

5. **Figure your income before taxes.** Subtract selling and general
   and administrative expenses from gross profit.

   At this point in time, you will not be able to estimate your income
taxes because the estimate depends largely on the form of business
you choose — sole proprietorship, partnership or corporation. Chapter 4 will help you determine which form is best for you and your
business.

Get Set . . .

Now that your business plan is drafted, you need to get the advice of an experienced business person to review it for content. If you do not know anyone who can do this for you, contact the nearest Small Business Administration office to speak with one of the experts in the SBA's SCORE program. Their help is free of charge.

Go!

Your business plan is drafted and checked for content. You need to take the last step to get it into a businesslike document for presentation.

Unless you are a trained editor, the best way to do this is to have a professional editor, publisher or business specialist make a final layout. They will edit it, lay it out in an attractive manner, type it and proof it, proof it, proof it. THERE IS NO ROOM FOR ERRORS, TYPOS OR SLOPPINESS HERE.

If you do not know anyone who can do this for you, look in the telephone book under secretarial services, editors and publishers. It may cost you a few dollars, but it will be more than worth it.

A Cork and Some Bubbles

Break out the champagne when your business plan is complete, because you truly will have mastered a monumental task. Just remember one thing. Even as the ink dries, your business and its environment are changing. Your plan, eventually, will have to change to keep pace.

Don't fret if elements of your plan are obsolete a few months down the line — that's what happens to all dynamic, growing organizations!

Your Road Map To Success
"i can." ™

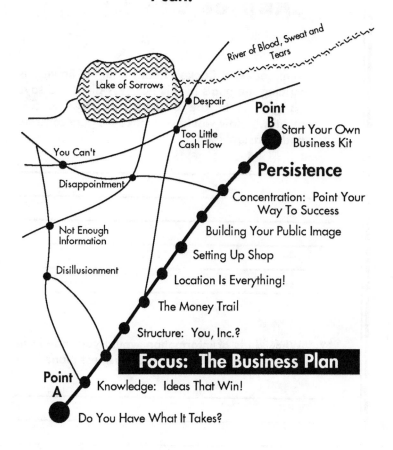

Chapter Checkpoint

1. Sam Cooke, of Cooke's Cooks Catering Service, is forming the goals for his business plan. He says his goal is to "be a success in three to five months." How would you make his goal concrete and measurable?

_____

_____

_____

_____

_____

_____

2. What kinds of information would you include in the operations section of your business plan?

_____

_____

_____

_____

3. What is the purpose of drawing up a balance
    sheet? How often should you draw up one for
    your business?

    _____

    _____

    _____

    _____

    _____

    _____

    _____

Notes

4

You, Inc.?

"Two are better than one, . . . for if one should fall, the other one can raise his partner up. But how will it be with just the one who falls when there is not another to raise him up?"

— *King Solomon*

Chapter Chart

Which form of business ownership is right for you? It's an important question, since the answer affects every other aspect of your business. This chapter presents the three major forms of business ownership, and explains the positives and negatives of each.

√ Sole proprietorship gives you maximum control of your organization but leaves you personally liable for bills and damages incurred by the company.

√ Partnerships offer better chances for adequate initial capital and spread the work among several people. They pose the risk, however, of power struggles, in-fighting, and personal liability.

√ Corporations minimize the problems of the other two forms of business structure. However, they can be difficult to set up properly, and they also require continuous attention to keep them running smoothly.

You, Inc.?

Introduction

One of your first jobs as an entrepreneur is to decide the legal terms of your ownership of the business — whether you're starting a neighborhood pizza shop or an interstate manufacturing concern with a budget in the millions. There are three major kinds of ownership recognized in the United States today: sole proprietorship, partnership and incorporation.

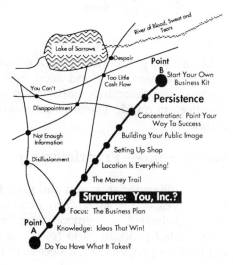

Your Road Map To Success
"i can." ™

River of Blood, Sweat and Tears

Lake of Sorrows

Despair

Point B Start Your Own Business Kit

Too Little Cash Flow

You Can't

Persistence

Disappointment

Concentration: Point Your Way To Success

Building Your Public Image

Not Enough Information

Setting Up Shop

Location Is Everything!

Disillusionment

The Money Trail

Structure: You, Inc.?

Focus: The Business Plan

Point A

Knowledge: Ideas That Win!

Do You Have What It Takes?

ABCs of Ownership

Sole proprietorship is by far the most common form of business structures, comprising more than 75 percent of the 18 million businesses operating nationally. But don't let that statistic fool you. Being in a solely-owned business is not always best. There may be serious drawbacks to a sole proprietorship.

In this chapter, we'll take a detailed look at the primary forms of business to help you make an educated decision about which form of ownership is best for you.

Forms of Ownership in the U.S.		
	Percent of Businesses	Percent of Sales
Proprietorships	75%	33%
Partnerships	8%	12%
Corporations	16%	51%

Before we get started, take a minute to consider some questions about what you want and need from your life in business. As we discuss proprietorship, partnership and incorporation, keep these questions in mind. The answers will determine your choice of ownership status.

Going Solo — Proprietorship

As a sole proprietor, you and your business are one and the same in the eyes of the law. You personally own all of the business's assets, including equipment, supplies and income. There are no complicated procedures to follow or reports to produce — you fill out licensing paperwork, if necessary in your locale, and go to work.

Factors To Consider When Choosing Your Form Of Business

Capital — How much money do you need to start up? Do you have it? How easily can you get it?

Risk — How much of your personal assets can you afford to risk to get the business started?

Tax Liability — What are you willing to do to minimize taxes on your earnings?

Control — How much control do you want? How much are you willing to share?

Privacy — Is it important to you that no one else know the innermost secrets of your business and finances?

Continuity — Does ease of ownership transfer of your business matter to you?

Ease and Cost of Organizing — How much time and money do you want to spend setting up ownership of the business?

Should you want to shut down your operation at any time, all you have to do is close your doors.

As a sole proprietor, you are in charge. You don't have to answer to anyone. If you wake up one morning with the burning desire to turn your fleet of gourmet ice cream trucks into bookmobiles, you may do so. Furthermore, you don't have to let anyone know of your plans — there are no public reports to file or partners to consult.

Many people choose to be sole proprietors because of the tax advantages. All profits from the company, since they belong to you, are taxed as your income, at your personal rate. You don't face the tax consequences of a corporation.

But there is a negative side of sole proprietorship. As you have more freedom in this structure, you also assume much more personal responsibility for the activities of your business. For example, you are personally liable for any and all debts that your company incurs.

Liability

If you can't sell your inventory of 30,000 red and blue widgets, you will have to pay for them yourself if your creditors make you. Or if your firm loses a lawsuit for injuries or damages, you will have to pay whatever judgements are against you. If you don't have the cash, your other assets — car, house, future earnings — could be taken as payment.

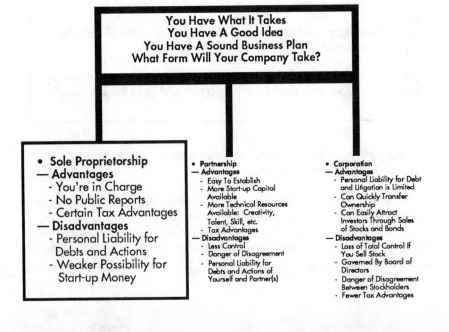

You Have What It Takes
You Have A Good Idea
You Have A Sound Business Plan
What Form Will Your Company Take?

- **Sole Proprietorship**
— **Advantages**
  - You're in Charge
  - No Public Reports
  - Certain Tax Advantages
— **Disadvantages**
  - Personal Liability for Debts and Actions
  - Weaker Possibility for Start-up Money

- Partnership
— Advantages
  - Easy To Establish
  - More Start-up Capital Available
  - More Technical Resources Available: Creativity, Talent, Skill, etc.
  - Tax Advantages
— Disadvantages
  - Less Control
  - Danger of Disagreement
  - Personal Liability for Debts and Actions of Yourself and Partner(s)

- Corporation
— Advantages
  - Personal Liability for Debt and Litigation is Limited
  - Can Quickly Transfer Ownership
  - Can Easily Attract Investors Through Sales of Stocks and Bonds
— Disadvantages
  - Loss of Total Control If You Sell Stock
  - Governed By Board of Directors
  - Danger of Disagreement Between Stockholders
  - Fewer Tax Advantages

Sole proprietors also find themselves with weaker possibilities for start-up capital than their organizational counterparts. A sole proprietor is the only person contributing to the support of the company, whereas partnerships have two or more. Corporations have any number, since a corporation's investors buy stock.

> **". . . For speed of start-up and autonomy of control, nothing beats the sole proprietorship. But if you intend to expand, hire employees, lease or acquire real estate, or take on significant amounts of payables, it will limit you."**
>
> **Paul Hawken**
> *Growing a Business*

Getting credit as a sole proprietor can also be difficult. If you are above average financially, you can get loans easily, but you have more to lose if things don't go well. If, on the other hand, you have few personal assets, you can't lose much, but you'll have a tough time getting the kind of money you'll need.

A Partnership: Two's Company

Partnerships are similar to proprietorships except they have two or more people in command. This structure is based on a document called the articles of partnership. It defines the terms of the partnership including the authority, rights and duties of each partner, the division of profits and losses, and what happens when a partner retires or dies. A sample Partnership Agreement is included in the **Start Your Own Business Kit** in the appendix.

Partnerships are almost as easy as proprietorships to establish. Your business can start operating as soon as the articles are signed by all parties. But partnerships offer some decided advantages over proprietorships that often make them an attractive alternative for entrepreneurs.

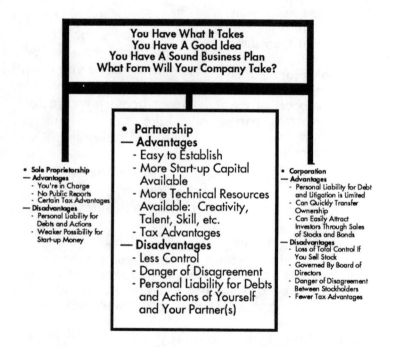

The fact that more people are involved means there are more resources available to the business — start-up capital, creativity, judgment, talent, skill — and an extra pair of hands to share the initial hard work.

Partners also can ease the loneliness many entrepreneurs feel during the first few years of operation, as they spend most of their waking hours making their dreams come true. It's easy to see why partners are the firm's most loyal, hardworking employees. Like you, they will do almost anything to keep their investment afloat.

Tax advantages to partnerships are numerous. In most income brackets, each partner pays less total income tax for profits than he or she would as sole proprietor. This is because profits are divided among partners and then reported on their respective statements as personal income. The same profits would be taxed twice in a corporation (more on corporate taxes later).

There are drawbacks to partnerships, too. You give up the power to make decisions on your own. Instead, every decision must be cleared with all the other partners unless other arrangements have been drafted in the articles of partnership.

While the partners' shared investment in a firm is a positive force if all goes well, it creates one of the major disadvantages of a partnership: the danger of disagreement. Unless the articles clearly show that one partner has more power, say 51 percent of the vote in a two-person firm, your business may be stymied by a stalemate. While you and your partners are busy disagreeing, customers remain unserved, deliveries are left unshipped and employees don't work.

> ". . . Partners can be helpful— if you have the right partners. But finding the right partner, like finding a good husband or wife, isn't easy. Steer clear of partners unless you are positively certain they will definitely add some profit potential to your business."
>
> — Tyler Hicks
> *How to Start Your Own Business on a Shoestring*

Another disadvantage of partnerships is that, like proprietorships, they offer no protection from liability. The personal assets of you and your partners are vulnerable to seizure for debts or damages.

Riskier still, you are liable for debts your partners incur without your knowledge or consent. Obviously, it pays to know the integrity of your partners before you sign anything.

Limited Partnerships

One way out of the liability is the limited partnership. In this arrangement, some partners assume unlimited liability for the firm's debts while others are liable only to the extent of their investment. The limited nature of some partners' participation must be clearly stated in the articles or all partners are assumed fully liable by the law.

Partnerships have one final drawback. They are valid only as long as all of the partners listed in the articles continue to participate. If one retires or dies, all agreements are null and void and new articles must be drawn up between the remaining partners. This is also true if a new partner is added to the group.

To Inc. or Not to Inc.?

If you're uncomfortable about proprietorships and partnerships at this point, you're not alone. Their disadvantages have long been recognized. In fact, they were what prompted Dartmouth College in 1819 to pursue legal recognition of a new kind of business organization: the corporation. Justice John Marshall defined the new entity as "an artificial being, invisible, intangible and existing only in contemplation of law." Corporations enjoy many of the rights and obligations that people do, including the right to sue and be sued and the ability to enter into contracts.

Corporations have several outstanding advantages that make them the ownership form of choice for many businesses.

First, your personal liability for debt or litigation is limited, except in rare cases, to the amount of money you've invested. Your personal assets are completely safe, as are those of other people who invest in your firm as shareholders. This factor alone makes it easier to draw investors into a corporation than into a partnership.

Second, you can quickly and easily transfer your ownership without having to dissolve the corporation. All you have to do is sell your shares of stock. And should you die, the corporation continues to exist and your shares can be passed on to your heirs as part of your estate.

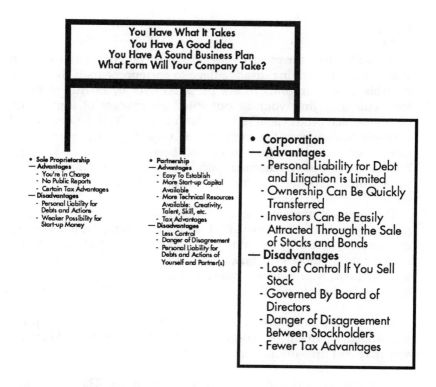

You Have What It Takes
You Have A Good Idea
You Have A Sound Business Plan
What Form Will Your Company Take?

• Sole Proprietorship
— Advantages
  - You're in Charge
  - No Public Reports
  - Certain Tax Advantages
— Disadvantages
  - Personal Liability for Debts and Actions
  - Weaker Possibility for Start-up Money

• Partnership
— Advantages
  - Easy To Establish
  - More Start-up Capital Available
  - More Technical Resources Available: Creativity, Talent, Skill, etc.
  - Tax Advantages
— Disadvantages
  - Less Control
  - Danger of Disagreement
  - Personal Liability for Debts and Actions of Yourself and Partner(s)

• Corporation
— Advantages
  - Personal Liability for Debt and Litigation is Limited
  - Ownership Can Be Quickly Transferred
  - Investors Can Be Easily Attracted Through the Sale of Stocks and Bonds
— Disadvantages
  - Loss of Control If You Sell Stock
  - Governed By Board of Directors
  - Danger of Disagreement Between Stockholders
  - Fewer Tax Advantages

The continuity of corporations is another factor that makes it easier to attract investors, because there is minimal danger of sudden interruption or dissolution due to personal factors.

There are other financial advantages to the corporate form. Corporations have the potential to gather a larger pool of money by offering stock to a larger base of initial shareholders or raising the price per share.

Later, corporations can raise capital by selling reserves of stock to new or existing shareholders. Corporations can also issue bonds which allow them to raise money while garnering precious tax advantages.

Loss of Control

As with other forms of ownership, incorporation has its down side. The most striking disadvantage to entrepreneurs is the loss of control. Since corporations are presided over by boards of directors, you may find yourself out-voted on matters of importance such as which products to sell or whom to hire. You may even find yourself ousted from the company, as was Stephen Jobs of Apple Computer, Inc. Even though he had been the brains and energy behind the company's dramatic success, the board decided the company would be better off without him and let him go.

The ease of transferring a corporation's ownership can also present problems. You may find yourself dealing with unsavory characters whose only recommendation is that they put up a considerable pile of money to buy stock. Unless you have some way around them, you have no choice but to live with them and their opinions on how to run the company.

One way to minimize your risk of losing control is buying the majority (51 percent or more) of the company's stock. Otherwise you may end up working for someone else.

Corporations are also noteworthy as tax traps. This reputation stems from the fact that Uncle Sam and the state tax the corporation on its profits, and tax the same money again as personal income when it is distributed to shareholders as dividends. In addition, the corporation must pay payroll taxes, property taxes and other asset taxes.

Chapter S

There are a few ways of easing the tax burden for corporations. First, if a company has 35 or fewer stockholders, it may be eligible for Chapter S status. This allows profits to be distributed immediately to shareholders and taxed only once as their personal income, much like taxation in partnerships. Though this tactic is useful for federal tax purposes, states do not recognize Chapter S. Unfortunately, traditional corporate tax procedures apply at that level.

Bonds

The other method of minimizing taxes is issuing bonds. A bond is a statement of indebtedness from a corporation to a person or other entity that has loaned the corporation money. Since interest payments on loans are a pre-tax deduction, they lower the corporation's net income and result in lower taxes.

> " . . . There are probably more 'family' corporations in the United States than any other kind. This type of business typically consists of the small, independent owner, whose partner helps out part-time and whose children or relatives also contribute some services."
>
> — Edward Siegel
> *How to Avoid Lawyers*

Birth of a Corporation

A corporation is established as an entity according to a charter, also known as its articles of incorporation. The charter is filed with the Secretary of State in the state where the corporation is headquartered and in any other state in which it wants to do business.

Corporations are governed by their bylaws which outline all of the activities involved in maintaining the corporation. They cover issuing stock, electing board members and paying dividends. The bylaws don't have to be filed with the state, but they should be drawn up at the same time as the charter. This eliminates the possibility of contradiction in the details of the legal entity being formed. Sample forms of articles of incorporation and bylaws are included in the **Start Your Own Business Kit** in the Appendix.

Corporations possess a unique name and seal which identifies the company to the public and on legal documents. If you choose a name that's already been used in your state or has national recognition value, your Secretary of State will require you to choose another. You also must include the word "company," "corporation," or "incorporated," or an abbreviation of them, as public notice of the firm's legal status. In some states you may also use the word "limited."

Finally, corporations issue stock certificates which are distributed to shareholders in exchange for money or other assets. Each certificate shows the shareholder's name, the number of shares owned and the price per share. Your Secretary of State will have information on where to obtain stock certificates locally.

Taking Stock

Corporations are owned by people — the people who purchase shares or stocks. Most stock is called common stock which means that every share carries with it the right to one vote in elections and matters of policy. Each also carries the right to share in the earnings of the corporation when dividends are declared and in assets in the event the corporation is liquidated.

You alone, or you and your associates, decide before incorporation on the number of total shares the company will issue. You also decide how many of the total shares will be made available for purchase and the price of each share. For a small business, it isn't necessary to create a large number of shares. In fact, many states levy a filing fee on a per-share basis, making it cheaper for you to create fewer shares. One hundred shares is more than adequate for most small businesses.

Next, decide how many shares to offer for sale. It's a good idea to keep a third to a half of the shares in reserve. This way, should you want to raise more capital later, you have shares to sell. Or, if you want to give a bonus to an employee, you can give him or her stock instead of precious cash.

Finally, decide the selling price of each share. The price of a share is called its par value and can be easily calculated using the following formula:

$$\text{Capital Needed} \div \text{No. of Shares for Sale} = \text{Price per Share}$$

Bread and Flowers Bakery, Inc. in Boulder, Colorado, is one example. Founder Monica Goldmund knew she needed $20,000 to start her business. To keep things simple for herself and her accountant, she created 500 shares of stock, kept 100 in reserve and offered 400 for sale. The price per share was:

$$\$20,000 \div 400 = \$50 \text{ per share}$$

Monica used her own capital to buy about half of the shares and sold the rest to investors and a local development organization.

As you may know from watching the stock market, the price of a share can fluctuate once it has been established. If in six months your company has exceeded everyone's hopes and dreams for turning a profit, one of your stockholders may sell his or her stock for double, or even triple, its par value. The selling price then depends on speculation about how much money each share will pay in dividends somewhere down the line.

The only limit to the number of shares a person can own is the number of shares initially made available. In other words, you might initially offer 100 shares of stock at $50 per share. How you sell the stock is entirely up to you. You might ask your friends and relatives to buy a share or two or you might buy 51 yourself and sell the balance.

Solo Stockholding

In most states you can legally own all the shares of your corporation. Some states require three shareholders at the initial incorporation but allow you to buy out the other two right afterward. As sole shareholder with rights to vote and share in dividends, you have much the same control as a sole proprietor with none of the risk.

Ready, Set, Go!

Once you've filed your charter, developed your bylaws and sold stock to shareholders, you can begin operating the corporation.

The first thing to do is to have the shareholders elect a board of directors. In a small corporation, the shareholders often double as board members along with the corporation's lawyer, accountant, and perhaps a key employee.

The board then appoints company officers and makes decisions for the company. These decisions are primarily policy decisions: Which projects to pursue; how to finance operations and growth; when to distribute earnings to shareholders, and authorizing the purchase of major assets.

The board of directors is required by law to meet at least once a year and to keep minutes of every meeting. Don't skimp on the minutes because their documentation could be important in possible litigation in the future.

Major resolutions passed at each meeting should be carefully noted. Although the minutes can't include every decision, they should always cover authorizations to enter into contracts or to sell or purchase real estate or other big-ticket items.

If during the year, an issue comes up that needs quick action, it is customary to call a special meeting of the board. If the corporation wishes to take out a mid-year bank loan, for example, the board must sign an authorization to borrow or the bank won't release a penny. Or if you find that a specific policy isn't working and you want to revise it, you'll want to call a meeting to discuss the policy and brainstorm ways to improve it.

Now that you've educated yourself about the various ownership options available to beginning entrepreneurs, take another look at the list of questions at the beginning of the chapter. All things considered, what are your priorities regarding capital, control, taxes, privacy, ease and cost of set up, liability and continuity? Only you can tell which form of ownership will be easiest for you to live with. So go ahead and choose!

You Have What It Takes
You Have A Good Idea
You Have A Sound Business Plan
What Form Will Your Company Take?

* **Sole Proprietorship**
— **Advantages**
 - You're in Charge
 - No Public Reports
 - Certain Tax Advantages
— **Disadvantages**
 - Personal Liability for Debts and Actions
 - Weaker Possibility for Start-up Money

* **Partnership**
— **Advantages**
 - Easy To Establish
 - More Start-up Capital Available
 - More Technical Resources Available: Creativity, Talent, Skill, etc.
 - Tax Advantages
— **Disadvantages**
 - Less Control
 - Danger of Disagreement
 - Personal Liability for Debts and Actions of Yourself and Partner(s)

* **Corporation**
— **Advantages**
 - Personal Liability for Debt and Litigation is Limited
 - Can Quickly Transfer Ownership
 - Can Easily Attract Investors Through Sales of Stocks and Bonds
— **Disadvantages**
 - Loss of Total Control If You Sell Stock
 - Governed By Board of Directors
 - Danger of Disagreement Between Stockholders
 - Fewer Tax Advantages

Your Road Map To Success
"i can." ™

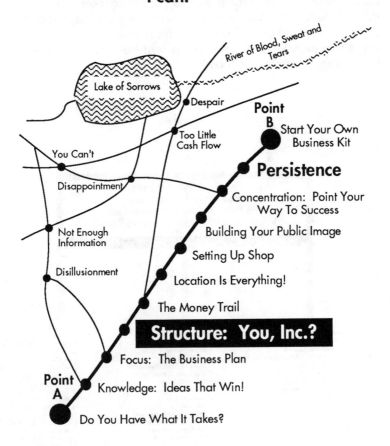

Chapter Checkpoint

1. What are the three major forms of business ownership practiced in the United States today?

   _____

   _____

   _____

2. Which of these forms offers owners the greatest protection from personal liability during the life of their business?

   _____

3. Name three disadvantages of working with partners in a partnership. Are there ways to minimize these disadvantages?

   _____

   _____

   _____

   _____

   _____

4. Is it legal for a person to own all of the stock in a corporation? If so, what advantages are associated with this arrangement?

_____

_____

_____

_____

_____

Notes

Notes

5

The
Money
Trail

"If you would know the value of money,
try to borrow some."

— *Benjamin Franklin*

Chapter Chart

How will you finance your life in business? This chapter shows you where to look for start-up capital and how to play the banking game and come out on top.

√   **Many people start with the money they can scrape together from their own savings and money from their friends and family.**

√   **Government agencies, venture capitalists and finance companies each have something to offer the new business owner in search of capital.**

√   **Not all banks are created equal. Some are truly helpful while some are like sharks in the water. You can learn to tell the difference.**

The Money Trail

Introduction

Your business cannot begin without money. You need to secure a location, hire employees, stock your shelves and advertise — all before your first customer walks in the door. Unless you are sitting on a pile of money, you will have to find the funds you need to start your business.

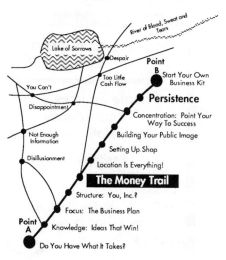

River of Blood, Sweat and Tears

Lake of Sorrows

Despair

Point B — Start Your Own Business Kit

Too Little Cash Flow

You Can't

Persistence

Disappointment

Concentration: Point Your Way To Success

Not Enough Information

Building Your Public Image

Setting Up Shop

Disillusionment

Location Is Everything!

The Money Trail

Structure: You, Inc.?

Focus: The Business Plan

Point A

Knowledge: Ideas That Win!

Do You Have What It Takes?

While it's true that banks are a significant source of loaned money, they are not the only or the most desirable source available. You also can obtain money from venture capitalists, finance companies, government agencies, friends and relatives — often on more favorable terms than a bank can offer.

Piggy Bank Financing

Countless businesses have been started with the owner cleaning out his or her savings account, adding small contributions from relatives, friends and neighbors who are willing to make a loan on the merits of your relationship. If you can generate enough money to get off the ground this way, by all means do so. It's the most accessible type of financing around, and it has the added benefit of making your friends and family feel good about being able to help you.

The major problem with this kind of financing is that you usually cannot generate an ample supply of money — you may have to live and work at near-starvation levels to make ends meet. Further-

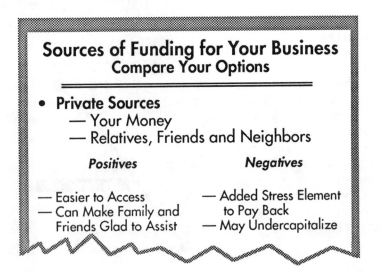

Sources of Funding for Your Business
Compare Your Options

- **Private Sources**
  — Your Money
  — Relatives, Friends and Neighbors

Positives	Negatives
— Easier to Access	— Added Stress Element to Pay Back
— Can Make Family and Friends Glad to Assist	— May Undercapitalize

more, you are temporarily living off of your friends' goodwill and you may feel considerable pressure to pay back your debts faster than you can afford to.

Some entrepreneurs in Kathy's position have solved their problem by taking out a bank loan a year or so into operation and using the money to pay back initial investors. A banker is more likely to loan you money once you have a history of sales and sound management.

Government Funding

> *Kathy Casadei, owner of The Compleat Jeweler in Santa Fe, New Mexico, used piggy bank financing. A year ago she scoured the pockets of relatives and friends to finance the gala opening of her pricey jewelry shop. Though business has been good, Kathy still has a long way to go before she can settle her debts. Because Kathy is so close to her creditors, she wants to pay them back now. "I know my Aunt Mary would buy a new car if she had her $3,000 back," she says. "Sometimes I feel like handing it over no matter what it does to my cash flow."*

Governmental agencies can often prove a reliable and accessible source of funding. At the top of the list is the Small Business Administration (SBA) which can provide loans at moderate interest rates or can guarantee loans made by banks. In a loan guarantee, the SBA promises to pay the bank in case you default on the loan.

Though SBA loans and guarantees are becoming more scarce in these days of social program spending cuts, it pays to check out this potential source of income. You can obtain a list of SBA offices around the country by writing to the SBA, Office of Public Information, Room 100, 1441 L Street, N.W., Washington, D.C. 20416.

State, county and community agencies sometimes offer loans to small businesses at attractive rates. These loans are often contingent

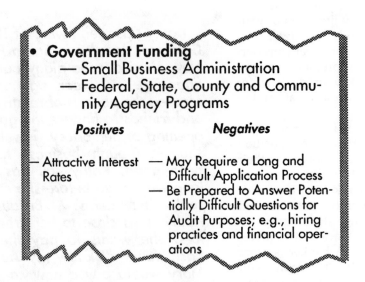

• **Government Funding**
   — Small Business Administration
   — Federal, State, County and Community Agency Programs

Positives	*Negatives*
— Attractive Interest Rates	— May Require a Long and Difficult Application Process — Be Prepared to Answer Potentially Difficult Questions for Audit Purposes; e.g., hiring practices and financial operations

on the location or type of business being started. In our community, businesses wishing to locate in a specific three-block area qualify for attractive start-up loans because the county is trying to revitalize commerce there. While qualifications for these loans vary widely, a little legwork on your part can land you a hefty chunk of money with few strings attached.

Finance Companies

Finance companies advance money to less mature businesses than commercial banks do. New business owners find that finance companies are a last resort for funding. They determine loan eligibility on assets rather than credit histories and income projections.

While borrowing money against your assets can be an advantage in some situations, it is also very risky. You may lose everything if your business is not successful.

Finance company money is also more expensive than bank money. The reason is simple: The company knows you can't get

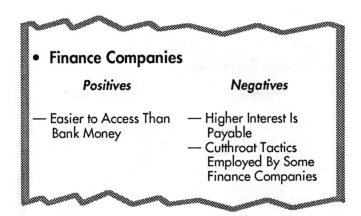

• **Finance Companies**

Positives	*Negatives*
— Easier to Access Than Bank Money	— Higher Interest Is Payable — Cutthroat Tactics Employed By Some Finance Companies

the loan elsewhere, and it will charge you whatever interest rate it wants.

Some business advisers recommend avoiding finance companies entirely because of their cutthroat tactics. This policy is a little extreme. If you find you need to work with a finance company, proceed with extreme caution. The specifics differ from company to company, so be sure to carefully check — with a lawyer's help — all the terms of the agreement before you sign anything.

Venture Capitalists

Venture capitalists are private investors who provide seed money to new businesses with exceptional growth potential. Investment firms, large industrial companies, insurance companies, trust funds and wealthy individuals are potential sources of venture capital.

Venture capitalists differ from banks in that they seek to protect their investment by asking for a degree of control over the business. They may want input into managerial decisions. Or they may want complete control of the company if certain financial objectives are not met by a certain date. A useful rule of thumb is that the more capital an investor risks on your business, the larger share of control he or she will expect in return.

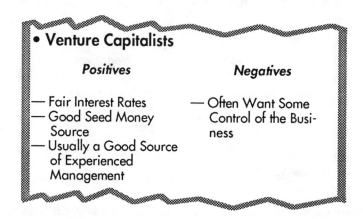

Many venture capitalists are highly experienced in new business management, having been part of many ventures in a relatively short span of time. Most business owners who use venture capital quickly recognize their investors as a resource for a wide range of financial and managerial matters. Not only do these owners obtain capital, but they get easy access to expert advice whenever they need it.

Attracting Venture Capital

For venture capitalists to seriously consider investing in your firm, they must be convinced that their money will see a phenomenal rate of return. Phenomenal, in this case, translates to the neighborhood of 35 to 50 percent per year. You have to be willing to work hard to make the profits that allow you to pay venture capitalists that kind of return. If you have the energy, they have the money to back you!

A national directory of venture capitalists, with information about each, is available from the National Venture Capital Association, 1655 North Fort Myer Drive, Suite 700, Arlington, Virginia 22209. You might also find sources of venture capital in business magazines such as *Venture* and *Inc.*, or in your local business tabloid.

The Banking Game

Banks are definitely the old standby in the world of business financing. The best among them deserve their reputation as community builders, helping businesses and individuals prosper through sound money management. Unfortunately, some banks think that they are doing you a favor by providing services.

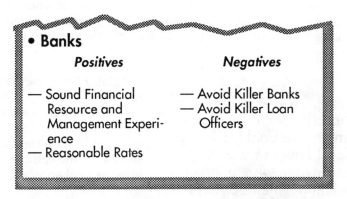

• Banks

Positives	*Negatives*
— Sound Financial Resource and Management Experience	— Avoid Killer Banks
— Reasonable Rates	— Avoid Killer Loan Officers

Since your investor is going to be in your life a long time, it pays to know what kind of institution or individual you are dealing with. Familiarize yourself with a number of banks in your area to get a feel for whether they operate with concern for their customers and the larger community or for profit alone.

Killer Banks

Killer banks are profit pirates. They lend freely when interest rates are low and call back their loans — in full — as soon as interest rates rise. Then they lend the money out again at a higher rate of interest.

One experience with a killer bank can be a blow to a small business owner. To identify killer banks, consult a lawyer, accountant or banking insider who knows the reputations of banks in your community.

Loan Officers

The other way to get a picture of your bank's orientation is to sit down with one or more of its loan officers and discuss your plans. Are the loan officers patient and friendly? Are they knowledgeable about the local business climate? Have they funded businesses of your size before? Are they willing to be frank about whether they think your business will succeed?

Try asking your loan officer for advice about your financing options. If he or she is responsive and genuinely interested in helping you, you have probably found a good place to do your banking.

> ". . . Never get the idea that a lender is doing you a favor. No banking institution I know of will do you or anyone else a favor. Lending is their business — and most of them are quite good at it."
>
> — Roger Fritz
> *Nobody Gets Rich Working for Somebody Else*

Think of the loan officer as the first gate-keeper between you and the piles of money in the vault. He or she can veto your application right away or send it to the committees that give the final approval.

However, you want a loan officer who will send your application to the committee only if he or she is convinced it will be approved. In the world of banking, having a credit application turned down is like getting a little black mark on your soul — you definitely want to avoid it at all costs. An astute loan officer can save you from this fate by advising you not to apply if your chances aren't very good.

Loan Lessons

Once you've found a place to borrow money and a loan officer you can work with, you're ready for the application process itself.

There are several things you should keep in mind as you journey down the money trail.

1. **Ask for more than you need.** If you need $40,000 ask for $50,000. Cover yourself. You don't want to run out of money because the market throws you a curve ball.

2. **Don't exaggerate.** Painting a fantastic portrait of your business potential will backfire. Your banker will quickly show you to the door. If you've followed the suggestions in Chapter Three, you won't need to exaggerate because you will have a solid, well thought-out plan that is sure to impress lenders. With your business plan, you can maintain unflagging confidence yet remain realistic about possible pitfalls.

". . . Where it was once enough to sit down at lunch and convince a banker that your boat would probably float, more often than not to gain the funds needed to launch your craft, you are now going to need a ship's log's worth of dot matrix."

— Thomas Jones
Entrepreneurism

Also, be realistic about your own credit history. It's futile to try to hide blots on your credit record; your banker will find them anyway. Be prepared to give good reasons for any difficulties you've had, and show how you've learned from the experience.

3. **Be realistic about repayment.** Don't agree to a repayment schedule that is unrealistic for your potential cash flow. Try to keep payments as low as possible or have them start out low and gradually increase over a few years. Nothing irks a banker — or ruins a credit record — faster than late or missed payments on a loan.

4. **Consider your banker's advice.** If your loan officer has suggestions that make your plan more appealing to the loan

committee, consider them seriously.   This person has been through the process countless times. You can benefit from his or her experience only if you are willing to listen.

5.   **Avoid giving a personal guarantee.** Most banks will want you to give a personal endorsement on a loan. They may even want your spouse to sign. This is too risky. If anything goes wrong, you could lose a whole lot more than your business.

6.   **Don't let rejection get you down.** Everyone is rejected at some point in business. Give yourself the chance to get mad, sad or worried, then pick up and go on.

A Final Word

A start-up business needs money like a seedling needs water. Your job as a beginning entrepreneur is to find the right amount of money at the right price under the right terms. With careful preparation and a proceed-with-caution approach, you can get what you and your business need to prosper. There are investors waiting for your call!

Sources of Funding for Your Business
Compare Your Options

- **Private Sources**
  — Your Money
  — Relatives, Friends and Neighbors

Positives	Negatives
— Easier to Access — Can Make Family and Friends Glad to Assist	— Added Stress Element to Pay Back — May Undercapitalize

- **Government Funding**
  — Small Business Administration
  — Federal, State, County and Community Agency Programs

Positives	Negatives
— Attractive Interest Rates	— May Require a Long and Difficult Application Process — Be Prepared to Answer Potentially Difficult Questions for Audit Purposes; e.g., hiring practices and financial operations

- **Finance Companies**

Positives	Negatives
— Easier to Access Than Bank Money	— Higher Interest Is Payable — Cutthroat Tactics Employed By Some Finance Companies

- **Venture Capitalists**

Positives	Negatives
— Fair Interest Rates — Good Seed Money Source — Usually a Good Source of Experienced Management	— Often Want Some Control of the Business

- **Banks**

Positives	Negatives
— Sound Financial Resource and Management Experience — Reasonable Rates	— Avoid Killer Banks — Avoid Killer Loan Officers

Your Road Map To Success
"i can." ™

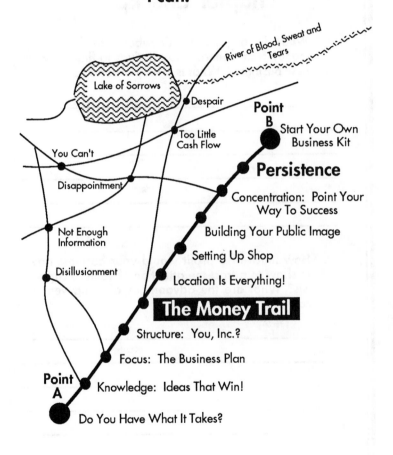

River of Blood, Sweat and Tears

Lake of Sorrows

Despair

Point B   Start Your Own Business Kit

Too Little Cash Flow

You Can't

Persistence

Concentration: Point Your Way To Success

Disappointment

Building Your Public Image

Not Enough Information

Setting Up Shop

Location Is Everything!

Disillusionment

The Money Trail

Structure: You, Inc.?

Focus: The Business Plan

Point A   Knowledge: Ideas That Win!

Do You Have What It Takes?

Chapter Checkpoint

1. What is a possible drawback to borrowing money from friends and relatives to finance your new business? What is a way around it?

   _____

   _____

   _____

   _____

   _____

   _____

2. How much of a profit would your business have to show to attract the attention of venture capital-ists? What are the advantages of using venture capital?

   _____

   _____

   _____

   _____

   _____

3. How can you tell if a certain bank is a good place to do business? How do you know if a loan officer will serve you well?

_____

_____

_____

_____

_____

_____

_____

Notes

6

Location Is Everything!

"A foolish man. . .built his house
upon the sand."

— *Matthew*

Chapter Chart

Location is a crucial factor in your success equation. This chapter outlines the challenges you face when choosing a location that's right for your business.

√ Your best location bargain may be your own home! Learn which kinds of businesses work well at home and which do not.

√ For retail shops and restaurants, the three most important survival factors are location, location and location — in that order. Knowing how to pick the best spot for your business is a survival skill you must learn.

√ If you can't afford your ideal location, you can still make a go of it. Learn how to beat the location game through effective advertising and promotion.

Location Is Everything!

Introduction

As you get closer to opening your business, you need to think about a very important question: where are you going to put it? Although this seems ridiculously fundamental, many would-be business owners often overlook it — and regret it later.

For some types of businesses, such as consulting firms, mail-order businesses or delivery services, location is important but not crucial. For others, including retail shops and restaurants, location is so impor-

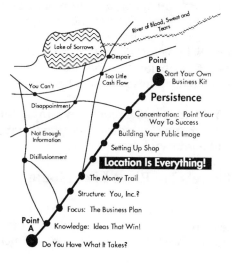

Your Road Map To Success
"i can." ™

River of Blood, Sweat and Tears

Lake of Sorrows

Despair

Point B
Start Your Own Business Kit

Too Little Cash Flow

You Can't

Persistence

Disappointment

Concentration: Point Your Way To Success

Building Your Public Image

Not Enough Information

Setting Up Shop

Disillusionment

Location Is Everything!

The Money Trail

Structure: You, Inc.?

Focus: The Business Plan

Point A

Knowledge: Ideas That Win!

Do You Have What It Takes?

tant that it may be the deciding factor in whether the business survives.

A Penny Saved . . .

One of your major priorities as a new business-owner is to reduce costs wherever you can. In addition to labor costs, you're going to have four major expenses:

1. Rent
2. Equipment
3. Inventory
4. Promotion

The more you can save on rent and equipment the more you'll have for inventory and promotion: two things important to your survival in the first couple of years.

Before you spend a lot of money on plush office space, first class furnishings and state-of-the-art equipment, consider that there may be a less expensive way. A study by the Suffolk University Business School found that 92 percent of new businesses could have started with lower expenses for rent, equipment and supplies — with no drop in sales and a healthy jump in profits.

You don't make money by simply throwing money around. You make money by judiciously *investing* it when and where it's needed. Cut corners where you can.

There's No Place Like Home

One start-up location is right underfoot. If you start your business in your home, you avoid paying extra rent and being locked into a lease before you know how much money you can make.

You also save on taxes. Part of your rent, utilities and other bills are legitimate business expenses. If you use 25 percent of your home for your business, for example, you can claim 25 percent of your home expenses (rent, utilities, etc.) as tax deductions. Just be sure you can document your use of that portion of your home for the business only.

Finally, you save money and time every day because you don't have to commute. This is especially important in urban areas where traffic, exhorbitant parking fees, and late trains are a fact of life.

> ". . . You may have to start out on the kitchen table or in a corner of the living room. Millions have started the same way and that's okay— for a while. To make the most out of working at home, though, you'll need to begin planning ways to make your working space more comfortable, efficient, and permanent."
>
> —Lynie Arden
> *The Work-at-Home Sourcebook*

Before you set up a business at home, find out about local zoning ordinances. If you live in a rural area, chances are you have nothing to worry about. But in populated areas, laws may prohibit certain kinds of businesses in residential neighborhoods to protect them from disruptive noise, traffic, odors or other nuisances.

Ten Best Businesses to Start at Home

- Courier and Messenger Services
- Catering and Party Planning
- Child and Elderly Day Care
- Carpentry Services
- Cleaning and Maintenance Services
- Mail-Order Retailing
- Visiting Nurse Services
- Dating Services
- Aerobics and Exercise Instruction
- Tour Guide Services

Working at home presents some unique problems. The border between work and your personal life may get fuzzy. You may find yourself sneaking

Possible Locations to Consider for Your Business

- **Home**
  - **— Positives**
    - Avoids Extra Rent Payment
    - Possible Tax Write-off
    - Saves Commuting Expense

  - **— Negatives**
    - Possible Conflict With Neighborhood Zoning Laws or Restrictive Covenants
    - Space May Be Limited
    - Easier To Be Distracted
    - Less Professional Image

away to deal with family matters, personal phone calls or a suddenly important snack — at great cost to your efficiency.

There may be a question of space. If you work in the midst of your living area, the time you spend setting up and breaking down operations every day could take away from your work.

Also, having your home double as an office might make you feel less professional. It can make your position as a newcomer more apparent and might give your customers the feeling that they are dealing with a fly-by-night operation.

Some of these problems are easily remedied. For about $15 per month, you can hire a prestige mail drop service and have a swanky address. For about $50 to $75 per month you can rent office space for an hour or two — for meetings with key customers.

- **Bargain Offices**
  - Office Basements
  - Small Sales Offices
  - Older Homes
  - Boarded-Up Commercial Property

Onward and Upward

There will come a time, perhaps sooner than you think, when your business will outgrow your home. Inexpensive and adequate office space may be difficult but not impossible to find. Commercial real estate agents usually avoid budget properties — to make higher commissions they need to close pricier deals. To find bargains you have to look for them, but the time spent searching can pay for itself in the long run.

Office basements can be bargains. Many businesses ready for expansion start by splitting their operations. They rent presentable office space for sales purposes and house the rest of their operations in the basement.

Older homes can be made into inexpensive office space. Before you sign the lease, however, make sure that local zoning laws allow business to be conducted in the area. Don't get stuck with unusable space!

It pays to be innovative. Spaces such as boarded-up gas stations, diners, and factories often can be renovated at low cost. Sometimes the building's owner will finance the work to attract tenants.

Where the Customers Are

Business experts rarely agree on anything. One thing they all believe, however, is that the three most important factors in the survi-

survival of a retail business are **location, location** and **location** — in that order.

Cheap is out, expensive is in if you're planning a retail start-up. Finding your prime location takes some research. Let's take a look at the factors to consider as you shop for your prospective site.

Greener Pastures

The first thing to consider is whether to locate your business in your home town or seek greener pastures. While personal preference should be a big factor in your decision, you also should consider whether your target area can support the kind of business you'd like to start.

> *Ray's Bait and Tackle in his home town of Nags Head, North Carolina, is located in the middle of prime fishing territory. But if Ray was from the Arizona desert, he might have had to move to find the client base he needs to support his business.*

Sometimes it's best not to leave your home turf. Contacts, especially in the financial community, are important. In your home town you undoubtedly have creditors who know you and a network of people who will help you get going. Your friends are your best first customers. Ask each friend to tell 12 people what a great service or product you provide.

Demographics

Demographics is Madison Avenue's term for finding out what the people in a certain region are like. As you know from your marketing study in Chapter Two, you need to know what the people in your target area need and want, how much money they make, whether they have kids, and so on. This information helps you judge whether they will be interested in your product or service and whether they can afford it.

In addition to getting the current picture of the people in your target area, you should also consider what the future will bring. Will certain kinds of people be moving in or out in the next few years? What kinds of products or services will they need or want?

Traffic Patterns

You can have a terrific idea, adequate financing, and a beautiful set up, and still fail. Why? Because you are located too far out of the way. You have to locate your business where customers will find you.

One way to find good locations for your business is to take a look around your target community. If you're in the city, you'll probably want to follow mass transit and walking routes. In the suburbs, you'll want to check out main thoroughfares and commuter routes.

> ". . . Subconsciously consider your customers as stupid and lazy. By lazy, assume they will not lift a finger to go out of their way to buy your product or service. By stupid, presume the customer is unable to read a map. The objective is to place the business in a location so obvious it cannot be overlooked."
>
> — James Halloran
> *The Entrepreneur's Guide to Starting a Successful Business*

Which routes seem reasonably busy? Are there landmarks that people pass frequently? Are there major attractions such as beaches, sports stadiums or parks? Wherever people already go is a good spot to do business.

Whether in the city or suburbs, you need to pay attention to parking. Never assume your customers will drive in circles looking for a parking spot just for the privilege of patronizing your store. Chances are they'll find another store that offers hassle-free parking.

> Even though Ray Kroc, founder of McDonald's, believes "saturation is for sponges," you ought to pay attention to this critical aspect of locating your business. Not all of us start out with an idea as irresistible as the one that propelled Kroc to fame and fortune!

Competition

It's vitally important to be aware of your competitors at all times. If you don't have a solid edge on them — in terms of price, quality or customer service — you'll want them to be well out of your way. For example, if you set up your hamburger stand between McDonald's and Burger King, you're asking for trouble. Your neighbors will surely out-advertise or under-price you until you're starved out.

Also, the number of people doing a particular business in an area is important to your success. Suppose your area contains seven drycleaning establishments, each of which is breaking even. Business moguls would say the drycleaning market in your area is saturated and unable to support further business. If you're hooked on the idea of being a drycleaner, you'd do well to look elsewhere for a home for your firm.

The Company You Keep

Not all of your neighbors are your competitors. Some neighbors may have a beneficial effect on your business. Locating near a popular department store, for example, practically guarantees a large volume of traffic in the vicinity of your store. Many a shopping mall has been built around one or two major department stores — whose large clientele then becomes available to the smaller surrounding stores.

> Milo Barrari put his Casa di Roma pizza shop next to the local movie house. People coming to see a movie could also enjoy a solid meal and a nice evening out.

Certain combinations of businesses can maximize each other's profits.

> • **Retail Offices**
>   — Is Prime Location Needed?
>   — Is Home Town Best Location?
>   — Consider Your Target Area:
>   - Traffic Patterns
>   - Customer Parking
>   - Saturated Market?

The maxim "You are judged by the company you keep" couldn't be more true in the retail business. The environment in which you work sends a strong message to your customers about the quality and price of your products.

Of course, businesses wishing to sell on the budget end of the spectrum wouldn't want to locate in Hannah's mall. Such businesses couldn't afford the overhead. Also, customers who buy budget products wouldn't shop in a pricey mall. These customers would prefer stores on the local highway strip where goods are priced and packaged to appeal to their sense of practicality, as well as to their pocketbook.

Hannah's Hosiery is a case in point. An upscale intimate apparel store, Hannah's is located in a refurbished turn-of-the-century train station in Washington, D.C. The station's ambience projects an image of quality — an image that enhances the businesses within.

Off the Beaten Path

Even if you find the perfect spot for your business, you may not be able to afford it. You may have to begin in a less-than-ideal location, but that is an obstacle that can be overcome.

One successful alternative to a high-priced location is to create a powerful, agressive and expert promotional campaign. Of course, this is costly, but you must let people know where you are. Hire a good advertising or public relations firm. Chapter Eight offers an excellent introduction to the world of promotion and explains how you can get the most out of your advertising dollars.

But even with the best promotion, you'll still need patience. It can take weeks, perhaps years, to build the reputation that brings customers to your door. Be prepared to wait.

Where to Get Help

When choosing your business location, you may have to search for what seems like a long time. A year or more is not unusual. You may want to consider hiring consultants that specialize in determining which locations best suit your retail needs. It's best to bring in consultants when you've narrowed down your choices to about two or three, so you don't pay for work you could do yourself.

Sources

Other places to go for help are your local Chamber of Commerce and your local office of the Small

> ". . . Learn to say no when a site doesn't meet your criteria. You just have to keep turning over rocks to find the worms. There are too many problems with low-volume locations, and too many opportunities for superstars, for you to take chances."
> — Philip Holland
> *The Entrepreneur's Guide*

Business Administration. These agencies specialize in helping businesses find good locations or professional assistance for locating a business.

Possible Locations to Consider for Your Business

- **Home**
  - **— Positives**
    - - Avoids Extra Rent Payment
    - - Possible Tax Write-off
    - - Saves Commuting Expense

  - **— Negatives**
    - - Possible Conflict With Neighborhood
        Zoning Laws or Restrictive Covenants
    - - Space May Be Limited
    - - Easier To Be Distracted
    - - Less Professional Image

- **Bargain Offices**
  - — Office Basements
  - — Small Sales Offices
  - — Older Homes
  - — Boarded-Up Commercial Property

- **Retail Offices**
  - — Is Prime Location Needed?
  - — Is Home Town Best Location?
  - — Consider Your Target Area:
    - - Traffic Patterns
    - - Customer Parking
    - - Saturated Market?

Your Road Map To Success
"i can." ™

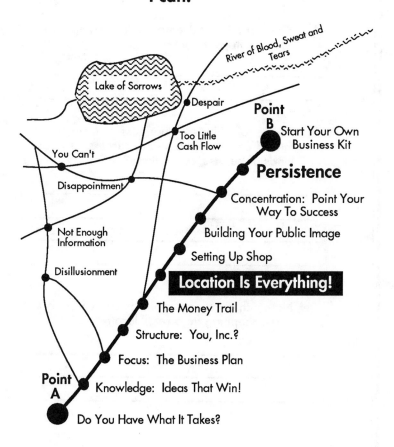

Chapter Checkpoint

1. What are two advantages to starting your business in your home?

    _____

    _____

2. For certain kinds of businesses, location is the primary factor assuring success. Which kinds of businesses are these?

    _____

    _____

    _____

    _____

3. Name three factors you should check out when shopping for a retail location.

    _____

    _____

    _____

4. How can you compensate for a less-than-ideal retail location?

_____

_____

_____

_____

_____

_____

Notes

7

Setting
Up Shop

"A miser is a person who lives within his income. He is also called a magician."
— *Robert Frost*

Chapter Chart

You've found your dream location. Now what? This chapter shows you how savvy business owners negotiate with landlords, get needed renovations, find furniture and equipment and begin operations.

√   No lease is final until you sign it. Learn how to negotiate with your landlord to get the best rent, security deposit and renewal terms for your business.

√   Renovations are often important considerations when you sign on to a site. Know whether your landlord will finance renovations — before you sign.

√   New business owners frequently overspend on furniture and equipment, which can cause a cash-flow crisis later on. Find out how to get furniture and equipment at rock bottom prices.

√   Well before you open your doors, you are involved in many financial transactions. Learn how to keep tabs on the money rushing in and out of your business's bank account, so you always know how much cash you have.

Setting Up Shop

Introduction

Setting up shop is more than putting a sign in the window and waiting for the customers to walk in. It also means negotiating favorable leases, getting needed renovations, and finding bargains in furniture and equipment. It means hiring employees and finding suppliers to provide you with merchandise and supplies. It means learning how to keep careful financial records of every business transaction you make.

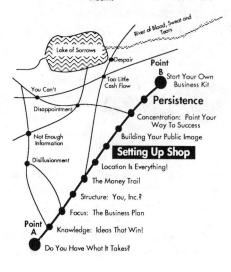

Your Road Map To Success
"i can." ™

River of Blood, Sweat and Tears

Lake of Sorrows

Despair

Point B Start Your Own Business Kit

Too Little Cash Flow

You Can't

Persistence

Disappointment

Concentration: Point Your Way To Success

Building Your Public Image

Not Enough Information

Setting Up Shop

Disillusionment

Location Is Everything!

The Money Trail

Structure: You, Inc.?

Focus: The Business Plan

Point A

Knowledge: Ideas That Win!

Do You Have What It Takes?

Working with Landlords

Unless you're going to work out of your home, one of the first steps to setting up shop is signing a lease on commercial office or retail space. The commercial lease is often lengthy and complicated, and it has an enduring impact on your bottom line. To protect your profits, you need to be familiar with and understand its terms and clauses.

> ". . . Renting is very elastic in terms of supply and demand. If the landlord is having trouble securing leases, or if your particular business would be an asset to his existing tenant mix, much of the lease can be negotiated. Too many inexperienced entrepreneurs fall victim to signing the lease as offered."
>
> — James Halloran
> *Entrepreneur's Guide to Starting a Successful Business*

All leases state a basic rent charge (per square foot of floor space per month); a security deposit to cover damages to the property during your occupancy and a duration requirement, usually three to five years but often longer. Most leases also describe your renewal options.

After these basics, leases can be specific about such things as the hours the business may operate, the kinds of merchandise that may be sold, and the kinds of insurance the tenant must carry.

Since the specifics vary from lease to lease and often appear innocent enough when written in strange and difficult language — legalese — it's best to show any lease you want to sign to a lawyer *before* you sign.

One more thing. Never be afraid to negotiate. Your landlord probably has an urgent need to get a tenant on the property.

Advertising and showing the property to potential renters is time-consuming and expensive. Moreover, he or she must pay the mortgage out-of-pocket when the property isn't generating rental income. You can use these facts to your advantage when negotiating options on your lease.

Let's look at the major components of the lease and discuss how you can turn each into an advantage on your road to success.

Rent

Sales are never so slow as when you first set up shop. You need to keep cash on hand to see you through these first lean months. One way to keep rent payments from gobbling up your limited cash reserves is to bargain for deferred rent.

In a deferred rent arrangement, you pay a lower rent during the first few months of the lease. In later months, when you can better afford it, you agree to pay a correspondingly higher rent. The net result is that you pay the same total amount of rent as you would in a regular rent arrangement, but payments are adjusted to make it easier for you.

Mitch Taylor, of Reno Contractors Inc. negotiated a deferred rent arrangement with his landlord. For the first 10 months of his lease, he paid $300 less per month than the regular $800 rent. For the following 10 months, he paid the regular figure. But during the 10 months after that, he paid the extra $300 per month back — making his monthly rent $1,100 per month. Therefore, he paid the higher rent at a time when he could better afford it — when his business was well-established.

How much can you negotiate on rent? It depends on the desperation level of your landlord. Landlords need cash like everybody else, and sometimes they face a cash crisis. If you're willing to risk losing the site, you could push the issue to see how much your landlord

will give in. We've known of truly desperate landlords giving up
to six months free rent — quite a savings for a little bargaining!

Security Deposits

Another item that can be negotiated to save you money when
you're starting out is the security deposit. Landlords routinely ask
for three to six months' rent for security deposits. With terms like
these, you can be priced out of an otherwise affordable location.

One way around the security deposit problem is to spread out
the payment over several months or to make it payable at a later
time. Another way is to pledge personal collateral, such as your
car or home equity, for an amount equal to the deposit. A
third way is to find someone to act as a guarantor, whose
liability is limited to the amount of the deposit.

> *Sally Martin of Falcon Cleaners combined the first and third options when trying to come up with her $1,500 security deposit. She asked her mother-in-law to assume liability for the amount for ten months. Then, five months into operation, she began paying the deposit in monthly installments of $300 until it was paid. Sally gained valuable time in her battle to save start-up cash.*

Duration and Renewal

A good location is hard to find, so you should keep yours
as long as you can. First, it's bad business to move.
Customers don't like searching for your new location.

Second, it's expensive to move with utility hookups, mover's fees,
and time taken from serving customers. Add the cost of changing
stationery, invoices and advertisements that have your old address
on them, and you've got a hefty sum.

The longer you keep your lease, the longer the period in which
your rent remains constant. Though your landlord will want cost-
of-living increases every year or so, these are nothing compared

with the way your rent would jump if you signed a   new lease elsewhere.

While three to five years is standard for commercial leases, longer is certainly negotiable. You'll save money and your landlord will be pleased by the thought of avoiding vacancies.

Renovations

Getting the renovations you need to begin operations in an optimal environment is an important step in setting up shop. Your job in this process is to make a list of the work that needs to be done and get reliable estimates on the cost of the work. Then you will be ready to negotiate with your landlord to finance the renovations for you.

The best time to bring up the subject of renovations is after you've shown that you are seriously interested in the property, but before you've signed the lease.   Until you sign you have bargaining power. After the deal is closed, your landlord has you — and any verbal promises not put into writing in the lease are unenforceable.

If you've asked for reasonable renovations and negotiated fairly with your landlord, you should get what you want without too much trouble. In case you run across an inflexible landlord, think carefully about whether you want this person in your life for several years. If he or she is inflexible now, how will he or she be over the next few years?

Legalese

Beware of legalese which may contain unfair terms and clauses. The most common of these is the percentage rent clause which entitles your landlord to a percentage of your profits if you exceed a certain sales volume during the term of the lease.

Say, for example, your lease has a percentage rent clause at the $100,000 mark. If you break $100,000 in sales your first year, you

Tips On Renovations and Your Landlord

• **Most seasoned landlords expect to make renovations for commercial tenants.**

• **It's his or her property. Renovation increases its value, which means a better return when it's rented or sold later on.**

• **Your landlord may be able to finance renovations by borrowing against the equity in the property.**

• **Avoid assuming the burden of financing renovations. Your new business needs to preserve your borrowing power — not renovate someone else's property.**

• **Watch out for back-door financing. Some landlords may try to overcharge you and make a profit on work you've requested!**

will have to pay a percentage of your yearly profits in addition to your regular monthly rent.

Protect yourself from legalese and other unwelcome surprises. Have a lawyer discuss every aspect of your lease with you. Don't skimp on lawyer's fees — they may save you money later on.

Furniture and Equipment

One of the most understandable mistakes new business owners make occurs when they begin decorating their office or retail space. Ordinarily prudent people often spend too much as they eye choice furnishings and imagine meetings conducted at mahogany-and-leather conference ensembles.

Cut corners where you can. Scour classified ads, auction notices and used furniture stores for bargains on the items you need. While it's easy to use a credit card and take home an office suite, doing so can cause trouble later.

One money-saver for new businesses is furniture rental. Renting is the equivalent of getting a loan, because you get the goods up front but you don't have to pay for them all at once. Over the long term renting is expensive, but for the first few months renting can help you avoid the lean look.

Some businesses find good bargains by snapping up furniture from franchises. To keep an up-to-date image, chains remodel often. The result is a surplus of moderately worn furniture and equipment, available for resale to start-ups. Keep an eye on the classified and business sections of your newspaper for information on bargains like these.

As you know from Chapter Six, many start-ups fail because they overspend on rent and equipment. Don't fall victim to this deadly business habit. Later, as profits mount and tax shelters become important, you'll have plenty of time for mahogany and leather.

Keeping the Books

One of the main chores in any business is bookkeeping. When you keep the books, you are maintaining a careful record of your daily cash flow. All money coming in — every check arriving by mail, every dollar put in the cash register — must be carefully noted. On the other end, every dollar going out —for payroll, supplies and overhead — must also be recorded. And if you're in retail, you must keep an accurate record of all inventory, which is really just cash in another form.

As you might guess, bookkeeping can be complicated. Growing businesses perform a hundred or more transactions every day. Nevertheless, you can learn to keep your books in a way that will satisfy the most exacting accountant .

It's not difficult, but it does take patience and a fondness for detail work. If you're the kind of person who hates hunching over an adding machine getting all of your columns to add up right, you may want to delegate your bookkeeping tasks to someone else. Find an accountant to take care of the books.

If you enjoy working with numbers, read on. In this chapter we'll present the two major forms of bookkeeping—single-entry and double-entry—and discuss the advantages and disadvantages of each.

Single-Entry Bookkeeping

Single-entry bookkeeping is easiest to set up and maintain, though not all businesses can use it. If you stock and sell merchandise, for example, you must use the double-entry method to conform to federal tax law.

Most likely, you already have experience with single-entry bookkeeping. You use it when you balance your personal checking account, for example.

In this method, also known as cash basis accounting, you record income when you receive it, and you record expenses when you actually pay them. You do not include money that is owed to you but hasn't been received, or money that you owe but haven't paid.

Track your cash flow in three categories:

• Income for month,
• Expenses for month and
• Balance

An example of single-entry bookkeeping may look like the chart on the next page at the end of each month: List the source, date and amount of all cash or checks received by the last day of the month. This is your income for month column.

Income

Date	Source	Amount	Balance
5/4/91	Item # 1	500.00	500.00
5/8/91	Item # 2	402.37	902.37
5/14/91	Item # 3	600.00	1,502.37
5/30/91	Item # 4	302.60	1,804.97

Then list the names of the payees, the date and the amount of all checks or cash paid out by the last day of the month. This is your expenses for month column.

Expenses

Date	Payee	Amount	Balance
5/1/91	Rent	700.00	700.00
5/13/91	Joe Clark	300.00	1,000.00
5/14/91	Paper Company	500.00	1,500.00

Next you figure the balance. Subtract your expenses from your income.

Income less Expenses, May 1990

Date	Payee	Amount	Balance
5/31/91	Total Income	1,804.97	
5/31/91	Total Expenses	1,500.00	
			304.97

If you have more income than expenses, you will have a positive balance. If you have more expenses than income, you will have a negative balance.

If the balance is negative, don't worry. The balance has little to do with your true profitability. It only shows what you have actually paid out or received for one month. You may have just closed a big deal but since your customer hasn't paid yet, the profits don't show up on paper.

In fact, you can expect your first few months to come up negative. It doesn't mean your business isn't sound, but rather that you are just starting and have more expenses than sources of income.

Not being able to see the relationship between cash flow and profitability is the critical disadvantage to single-entry bookkeeping. To get an accurate picture, you must use the slightly more complex double-entry method.

Double-Entry Bookkeeping

All double entry accounting is based on the accounting equation:

Assets = Liabilities + Capital

Assets are what a business owns. **Liabilities** are what a business owes, and **capital (or owners equity)** is the amount left when you subtract your liabilities from your assets.

Assets and liabilities can be measured directly. But you can't know what a business' capital, or equity, is until you know its assets and liabilities.

When it comes to recording transactions, classify all your finances into **accounts**. Accounts fall into two basic types: temporary and permanent (also called "real").

Temporary accounts exist only for a certain period (daily, weekly or yearly). These accounts are summarized in a financial statement, and "posted" (transferred) to ledgers to become part of the permanent accounts.

There are two kinds of temporary accounts: income and expense. **Income accounts** record the sale of goods or services and measure the inflow of assets, usually in terms of cash. **Expense accounts** record what a company spends or sells daily; they measure the outflow of assets in terms of cash and inventory.

Permanent accounts are carried over from one period to the next. They are "real" because they deal directly with assets, liabilities and capital.

Double-entry bookkeeping gets its name from the fact that for every business transaction made, entries must be made in at least two different accounts (one being a debit, the other being a credit), and the total amounts must be equal.

What are debits and credits? When you set up an account, in either a journal or ledger, the format you use will be two columns. Debits are entered on the left-hand side, credits on the right. In accounting, the terms debit and credit do not have the traditional meanings associated with them in banking — a debit decreases your account while a credit increases it. It is very important to remember that in accounting, the terms mean nothing more than:

Debit = Left Column Entry
Credit = Right Column Entry

"Why Keep Records?: How Good Information Keeps You In the Driver's Seat" (published by *Successful Business Management*), gives you some idea of what debits and credits mean.

Journals

Journals are called books of original entry because they are the first place in which you record transactions. Later, you make

Type of Account	To Show	
	Increase	**Decrease**
Asset Account	Debit	Credit
Liability Account	Credit	Debit
Capital Account	Credit	Debit
Revenue Account	Credit	Debit
Expense Account	Debit	Credit

entries recording the status of your accounts in ledgers, which are known as books of final entry. Your journals have two functions:

1. To provide a complete day-to-day record of similar transactions, classified under a common category.

2. To accumulate the results of daily transactions into periodic totals (usually monthly), so that these totals can be conveniently posted to the ledgers, the primary books of account.

In a new business, you may need just one journal — the **general journal** – to accurately and thoroughly record transactions. As your business expands, you will need several journals. These are special journals.

Special Journals are used when there is much activity in various accounts. Daily activity is recorded and periodically (for instance, once a month) summarized in the general journal.

For example, when you start out, you may write only a few checks per month. Those you do write will be entered as debits to the cash account in the general journal. A year later, you could be writing 150 per month. This is when you need to use a **cash disbursements journal**.

Likewise, you will be getting more cash receipts as your sales increase, so you will use a **cash receipts journal** and periodically enter the balances into the general journal.

It is typical for a small firm to keep five special journals and a general journal. These special journals are:

Journal	Type of Transaction
Purchases	Goods and Services Bought
Sales	Goods and Services Sold
Receipts	Cash or Checks Received
Disbursements	Cash or Checks Paid Out
Payroll	Wages, Salaries and Deductions

Typical Journal System

A typical financial journal consists of a record book divided into columns and rows. Across the top of each page, these column titles should be listed:

- date of transaction
- description of transaction
- debit column (left-hand side)
- credit column (right-hand side)

You will need at least three lines to record a transaction. The first line describes what is to be debited. Write the name of the account to be debited in the upper left-hand corner of the transaction description column; then in the debit column, write the amount to be debited.

On the next line of the description transaction column, indent about five spaces and enter the name of the account to be credited (to distinguish it from a debit entry). Then enter, in the credit column on the same line, the amount. On the third line, enter the description of the transaction itself. If there is more than one debit or credit, all the debits are listed first, then all the credits. A typical section of a small consulting firm's general journal is shown on the next page.

Date	Transaction	Debit	Credit
12/1/90	Stationery Cash, check 101 *Purchased Stationery*	100.00	100.00
12/5/90	Answering Service Cash, check 102 *Paid for answering service* *for November 1990*	65.00	65.00
12/15/90	Office Equipment Cash, check 103 Accounts Payable *Purchased copier and fax* *with cash and credit card*	100.00	50.00 50.00

Here are some examples of typical debit or credit entries in each special journal.

Ledgers

Ledgers record increases and decreases in accounts. Use them to track your financial status.

Information from your journals is posted to your ledgers as often as possible. The ledger where you keep your asset, liability, and capital accounts is known as your **general ledger**.

Journal	Typical Debits	Typical Credits
Purchases	Asset Accounts - Equipment - Goods and Services Bought - Inventory Expense Accounts - Office Supplies - Insurance	Accounts Payable Cash
Sales	Accounts Receivable Cash	Sales Sales Tax Payable
Receipts	Discounts Allowed Cash	Accounts Receivable Capital Contributions Sales
Disbursements	Accounts Payable Payroll Bank Charges Utilities	Cash
Payroll	Salary Expense Payroll Taxes Expense Cash	Payroll Taxes Payable

Since most businesses deal in credit, you may need two additional ledgers to handle items and expenses bought, borrowed, sold and loaned on credit.

- **Accounts payable ledger** contains the accounts of companies or people your business owes money to. Each supplier or creditor of your business usually is given a separate account.

- **Accounts receivable ledger** records the accounts of those who owe you money. Separate accounts are usually set up for each debtor of your business.

Total the balances of all the accounts in both ledgers at the end of each month. Summarize and post these balances in your general ledger under accounts called accounts payable (a liability account) and accounts receivable (a current asset account).

Your Financial Position:
Balance Sheets and Income Statements

Once a month, you need to do a financial summary. Prepare a **statement of financial position**, or a **balance sheet**. A balance sheet lists your asset, liability, and capital accounts, and the balances of each. Also, you need an **income statement** which lists all revenue and expense accounts and their balances.

Your income statement determines your profit or loss. If revenues exceed expenses, you have a profit and your capital rises. If expenses exceed revenues, you experience a loss and your capital goes down.

The Trial Balance

Before you do the balance sheet and income statement, prepare a **trial balance** to ensure that your account totals are correct.

To run a trial balance, list all your general ledger accounts with the amounts entered in a two-column, credit-and-debit format. After all accounts and their balances have been listed, total debits must equal total credits. If they don't, there is an error. In case of errors, check to see if there has been a mistake in posting to the ledger or in adding up the totals.

This chart shows how ledger accounts relate to your monthly (or quarterly) and end-of-year financial statements.

Financial Statement	Ledger Accounts
Balance Sheet	**Asset Accounts** Cash Petty Cash Accounts Receivable Office Furniture Office Equipment Stationery Inventory **Liability Accounts** Accounts Payable Notes Payable Mortgage Payable **Capital Accounts** Owner's Equity or Stockholders' Equity
Income Statement	**Revenue Accounts** Consulting Services Sales **Expense Accounts** Utilities Taxes Interest

Below is a typical balance sheet for a small business.

Joe's Pizza and Sub Shop, Inc.
Balance Sheet
December 31, 1990

Assets

Cash	$ 10,000
Petty Cash	1,000
Accounts Rec.	7,000
Notes Rec.	500
Equipment	8,000
Stationery	500
Buildings	50,000
Land	70,000

Total Assets   **$147,000**

Liabilities

Accounts Pay.	$20,000
Notes Payable	17,000
Mortgage Pay.	70,000

Capital

Stock Issued	40,000

Total Liabilities and Capital   **$147,000**

Joe's Pizza and Sub Shop, Inc.
Income Statement
Period Ending December 31, 1990

Revenue

Sales	$	9,000	
Services		1,000	
Total Revenue			$ 10,000

Expenses

Salaries	$	2,000	
Taxes		1,000	
Utilities		200	
Legal and Accounting Fees		300	
Consulting Fees		200	
Total Expenses			$ 3,700
Profit			6,300

If your expenses exceed revenue, you have incurred a loss for the period, and you would put the figure in parentheses.

Your financial statements must be complete and accurate because they are used to compute your taxes. Any error you make, no matter how small, can grow to unmanageable proportions if not corrected.

You should hire an accountant as soon as you can afford one. When you start out, an accountant may be needed only to set up the end-of-month and end-of-year income statements. You will find that the bookkeeping is best left to professionals so you are free to manage the rest of your business.

A Beginner's Guide
to Bookkeeping Terms

Account — A record of an individual asset, liability, revenue, expense or element of equity.

Accounts Payable — Amounts owed by a business for goods or services purchased on credit.

Accounts Receivable — Amounts owed to a business for sales or services performed on credit.

Credit — An entry in the right column of an account.

Debit — An entry in the left column of an account.

Journal — A chronological record of all financial transactions, entered daily.

Ledger — A record of financial transactions, taken from the journal, arranged by account.

Financial Statements — Documents providing financial information to users. They include the balance sheet and income statement.

Your Road Map To Success
"i can." ™

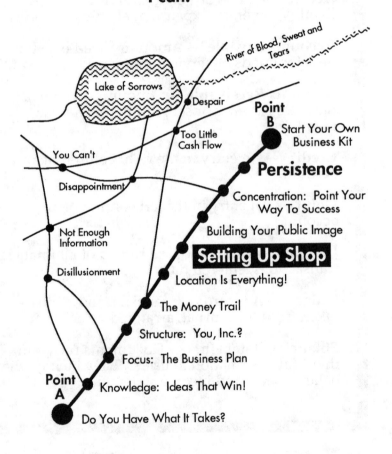

River of Blood, Sweat and Tears

Lake of Sorrows

● Despair

Point B
● Start Your Own Business Kit

Too Little Cash Flow

● **Persistence**

You Can't

Disappointment

● Concentration: Point Your Way To Success

Not Enough Information

● Building Your Public Image

● **Setting Up Shop**

Disillusionment

● Location Is Everything!

● The Money Trail

● Structure: You, Inc.?

● Focus: The Business Plan

Point A
● Knowledge: Ideas That Win!

● Do You Have What It Takes?

Chapter Checkpoint

1. When is the best time to bring up the subject of renovations with your landlord?

_____

_____

_____

_____

2. Name two good reasons why your landlord should finance the renovations.

_____

_____

_____

_____

_____

_____

3. How can you avoid overspending on furniture and equipment when you're just starting out?

_____

_____

_____

_____

_____

4. The two main forms of bookkeeping are single-entry and double-entry. How are they different?

_____

_____

_____

_____

_____

Notes

Notes

8

Building
Your Public
Image

"If you would not be forgotten as soon
as you are dead, either write things worth
reading or do things worth writing about."

— *Benjamin Franklin*

Chapter Chart

People have to know about your product or service to patronize your business. Through a combination of carefully selecting and building your image, drawing attention to your product or service and working hard to sell yourself and your dreams, you can develop a winning business.

√   Developing an image for your business is an important way to communicate to customers what your work is all about.

√   There are many forms of advertising, some more costly than others. A little strategy goes a long way toward helping you get your message out without emptying your pockets.

√   Publicity is another way to attract attention to your work and your products. Learn how you can write your way into the public eye or get reporters to do it for you.

Building Your Public Image

Introduction

People can't buy your product or service unless they know about it. And they won't buy it from you unless they have a good idea of what you and your company are like.

To get the customers you need, you have to draw attention to your product or service and carefully select and build your image. You have to work hard to sell yourself and your dreams.

Your Road Map To Success
"i can." ™

River of Blood, Sweat and Tears

Lake of Sorrows

Despair

Point B Start Your Own Business Kit

Too Little Cash Flow

You Can't

Persistence

Disappointment

Concentration: Point Your Way To Success

Not Enough Information

Building Your Public Image

Setting Up Shop

Disillusionment

Location Is Everything!

The Money Trail

Structure: You, Inc.?

Focus: The Business Plan

Point A

Knowledge: Ideas That Win!

Do You Have What It Takes?

What's Your Image?

The key to finding the image that will sell your business is thinking about who your customers are. You probably have a few good ideas about these people from the market study we discussed in Chapter Two. What are your potential customers like; what are their needs, their interests and their desires?

> ## Building Your Public Image
> ## Step by Step
>
> 1. **What Image Do You Want Your Business to Have?**
>   **Make Your Decision Based On:**
>   — **The Type of Business You Have**
>   — **Your Target Area**
>   — **Your Target Customers**

You have to project yourself into the minds of your customers. Once you do that, you can develop an image that will be irresistible to them.

Developing an image is easier than it sounds. Think of a business you know, a pizza shop, for example. What's its image? Probably casual, fast and friendly. Now think of an antiques dealer: a totally different image — professional, exclusive and expensive.

> 2. **Once You've Decided. . .**
>   — **Be Consistent**
>   — **Promote, Promote, Promote**

Be Consistent

Once you've found your market and worked out an image that sells, stick with it. If your market calls for a conservative image, go with it all the way. Don't hand out gray and navy business cards one day and fluorescent orange bumper stickers the next. People will get confused about what you stand for and will take their business to someone they feel they can trust.

Don't worry about laying it on too thick. The most successful organizations hold back nothing in promoting their business.

The Ad Game

Good, old-fashioned word-of-mouth always has been, and always will be, the most effective advertising of all. In fact, other forms of advertising are only substitutes for word-of-mouth.

Casey Magee of Quickie Print in Houston made up thousands of stickers with his business's name and number on them. He left a trail of smiles and stickers everywhere he went. People who shook his hand got a sticker on their palm. As he patted someone on the back, he left a sticker.

As hokey as his method sounds, it worked. People remembered Casey. And when they needed a printing job done fast, they called the little man with the big smile who left stickers everywhere.

But you have to satisfy a few customers before they can go around bragging about how wonderful you are. How do you find these first few customers? Advertising. How do you keep your customer base growing while your customers brag about you? Advertising.

Since advertising will be a fact of life as long as you operate your business, you need to know how to get the most out of your dollar. It helps to know what kinds of advertising is available to help you spread your message.

A Guided Tour of Advertising Media

When people talk about advertising, most think immediately of advertisements in newspapers or magazines. Advertising can also be telephone calls, banners on hot air balloons, handwritten letters, free pen-and-pencil sets and sales calls. In fact, anything can be a medium for advertising. Let's take a closer look at the options.

Direct Mail

In a direct mail campaign, you send a letter, brochure, catalogue or other printed material directly to people you think are interested in your product. You control exactly who gets the piece and you can offer a more detailed, reasoned pitch than you have space for in most other kinds of ads.

The drawback to direct mail is summed up in two words: junk mail. Many people assume that unsolicited mail is junk, and they throw away a large percentage of it unopened.

The trash factor notwithstanding, direct mail can be a powerful tool in a broad-based advertising campaign — especially if your business serves a specialized market. You can be reasonably certain, for example, that a tropical fish owner will read material promoting your new mail order company carrying merchandise for home aquariums.

The key to a successful direct mail campaign is narrowing the market to its thinnest slice. Then the people who get your material can't help but open the envelope and give your message a chance. When handled this way, direct marketing actually saves you money because you concentrate your ad dollars on the people who care most about your product.

Classified Ads

Classified ads provide an economical way of introducing your business to the community. Again, specialization is the key. Identify publications of interest to your target market. Anything from *Bee World*, the national magazine of beekeeping, to *Publisher's Weekly*, the national magazine of book publishing, can bring your specialized market to you.

Another variation on the classified ad is the display classified ad. Larger than a regular classified, it can be printed in boldface type, include your logo, and have a border. These ads jump off a page of dull three-liners. For slightly more money than a regular classified, display classifieds capture the attention of all who glance across the page.

Display Ads

Display ads are the workhorse of the advertising world. They are useful because they convey information not only through words, but also through graphic design elements which give a sense of your overall image. Some advertisements convey relatively little solid information, giving themselves over completely to image and style.

The mix of information and style in your display ads should be balanced by your business's needs, the clientele you hope to attract, and your overall advertising strategy.

One particularly economical trick, good for new businesses on tight budgets, is to let your firm's business card double as a small display ad. This is especially effective if the business card contains a compelling graphic, such as a line drawing or an interesting typeface, as part of the design.

It's often useful to include a coupon in your advertisement. By far the most common is the "Send for your free brochure/catalogue" variety. This device is very effective because anyone who sends in the coupon is a promising candidate for a sale and a good target for further promotional efforts such as direct mail.

Radio and Television

Be prepared to spend big if you want to use radio or television. Though costly, these media have a lot to offer your advertising effort. They reach many more consumers in one run than printed media can. They also have snob appeal. People know these ads are ex-

> "... Slice-of-life, demonstration, image, humor, tugging the heart — anything TV can do, radio can do better. Radio can put money into the entrepreneur's pocket quicker, because radio is the most immediate way to change consumer habits and practices, and, at the same time, demand a specific action at a specific time and place."
>
> — John Lyons
> *Guts: Advertising from the Inside Out*

pensive, so broadcast advertising lends prestige to your operation.

It's important to remember that broadcast ads reach a diverse audience. If your product appeals to a specialized market, you may be wasting money giving your pitch to thousands who won't respond. Make sure that broadcast ads will work for you before you spend your cash.

Telemarketing

Telemarketing is a form of advertising done over the telephone. Salespeople call individuals likely to be interested in your product or service and talk to them about what you have to offer.

3. Advertising Options
   — Newspapers, Magazines, etc.
   — Television, Radio
   — Direct Mail
   — Display Ads
   — Classified Ads
   — Business Cards, Printed Pencils, Cups, T-shirts, etc.
   — Catalogues, Brochures
   — Telemarketing
   — Signs, Posters, Billboards
   — Yellow Pages and Other Directories

Because this form of advertising involves direct interaction between a salesperson and a potential customer, it can be very effective. If the customer has misgivings or questions about your product or service, the salesperson can alleviate those doubts. If you want to emphasize certain aspects of your business — your superior warranty and return policy, for example — the sales staff can play up this part of your pitch.

Since the advent of the computer, a machine can sit at a desk, dial telephone numbers and deliver your spiel about your products and services. All the programming in the world, however, can't make the computer an eloquent, charming salesperson. Don't be tempted by lower cost into using automated telemarketers.

Location Ads

Location ads include posters, billboards and signs strategically located where large numbers of people will see them. This type of ad must be very noticeable — otherwise people will tune it out. Some business owners use the same artwork and design in both space ads and location ads. Not only does this save money, it also makes it easier for the public to associate a certain image with your business.

The crucial factor in developing a location ad is the location itself. How many people can see the advertisment without going out of their way?   Another important factor is the length of time your ad will stay in place. Your ad works much harder for you the longer you let it remain because more people have a chance to see it more times.

You see an effective location for advertising every day — the grounds of your business itself. If your building is visible to passersby, you could put a sign or awning outside to announce your business. Not only will you advertise your business, you'll also show that it is right there, where people practically trip over it on their way to other places.

The Trinkets of the Trade

Ron Sommers with Accutron Weather, Inc. in Athens, Georgia, promoted his forecasting service by handing out small thermometers on keychains at a national convention of meteorologists. Of course, meteorologists have a weak spot for thermometers — the promotion was a big hit!

Another time-tested method of advertising consists of handing out small articles that people use every day — matchbooks, pens, coffee cups, calendars and key chains that have your logo on them. Every time someone uses the article they will be reminded of your business.

It makes good marketing sense to match the trinket with the market you're going after.

The Yellow Pages

Probably the best bargain around for advertising is the one most often taken for granted: the *Yellow Pages*. Your business will have long-term exposure at a reasonable cost.

First, it reaches nearly every household, and it neatly guides consumers in search of your product or service directly to your ad. Second, your ad works for an entire year. Third, you won't find a less expensive space anywhere. So by all means, let their fingers do the walking!

The Personal Approach

As chief executive officer of your company, you have a lot of clout. You can use that clout in personal sales calls to well-targeted potential customers. Establishing a warm personal connection with key people practically guarantees that they will choose your firm when they need a product or service that you offer.

Don't use this contact to make a hard sales pitch. Instead, establish a business relationship, find out firsthand just what your potential customers need, and show them that your company is positioned to answer that need.

If you use this approach, keep a couple of points in mind. First, you have to be polished. If you're nervous or disorganized, you look like an amateur.

Second, make sure you're getting to the people who count. If your business is drafting supplies, present yourself to the art department, not to the receptionist. If, on the other hand, you have a courier service to sell, go straight to the secretaries who make the decisions about which courier to use.

Strategy and Your Budget

There's more to advertising than merely throwing dollars at a newspaper, television station or telemarketing company. You have to know how to make each dollar work as hard as possible to bring your customers to you. Sound advertising strategy helps you make the most of your advertising budget and strengthens your image within your market.

> **". . . Don't make the mistake of believing you get only one chance to reach your potential customer, or that each package or advertisement must tell everything. Much better to proceed as though you are beginning a long dialogue with your customer. Write copy that respects this relationship."**
>
> **— Paul Hawken**
> *Growing a Business*

Diversity

If you diversify, you hedge your bets on every ad you buy. If you sink your entire advertising budget into one space ad, and it is unsuccessful, you're out of money — and luck. It is better to combine a number of different types of ads in a well-planned campaign. If one ad doesn't work, you will have others that may.

Cost-effectiveness

You can spend $70 to get your name in the *Yellow Pages* or $15,000 for a 30-second spot on your local television network. How can you tell if the larger price tag is worth it? You need to look at two major factors: cost and effectiveness.

When thinking about effectiveness keep in mind the factors that can make or break your ad:

How many people will see it?
How often will they see it?
Will they respond to it?

The greater the number of people who see your ad, the greater the number who will be able to respond. Consider the billboard on your local thoroughfare or the half-page ad next to your local T.V. listings. Hundreds, perhaps thousands, of people see these ads on a given day. Think of the results if just one percent of these people respond to the ad.

Repetition

Research has shown that people like something better the more they're exposed to it. Repetition, therefore, is a cornerstone of successful advertising.

You achieve repetition by leaving your ad somewhere for a period of time. If you're running a display ad in your local newspaper, for example, run it for four issues instead of just one. Each time readers see it, they are one step closer to becoming your customer.

If your ad is on a billboard or poster slot, leave it there for several months. Let it penetrate the minds of passersby so that one day, when they need your product or service, they automatically turn to your company.

The Punch Factor

For an ad to sell, it has to have punch. It has to win people's attention over the messages of your competitors. Think about some ads you've seen lately. Chances are, you remember only one or two of the hundreds you've been exposed to. For your money, wouldn't you like your ad to be memorable?

Publicity — Read It in the Papers

The power of advertising is hard to dispute. But sometimes even advertising isn't enough. You can get an edge on the competition by combining advertising with well-placed publicity.

Publicity, unlike advertising, is free. Also unlike advertising, publicity is considered unbiased, for the simple reason that it comes out of editorial departments, under the careful review of editors who aren't on your payroll.

The best publicity comes from feature articles in local newspapers and magazines. Either you write the article yourself or you get a reporter to write it for you. Though it can be tricky to get a reporter involved, with a little savvy you can have all the coverage you need.

Feature Articles

As someone whose life is devoted to the business you run, you are an expert. You may take your know-how for granted, but what you know is valuable to other people.

Suppose, for example, your business is dry cleaning. You know a lot about fabric care, stain removal and quality treatment for long-lasting wear and durability.

To get publicity, you could write an article on what you know for your neighborhood newspaper. Two or three double-spaced pages would be plenty. Readers of the article would get the impression that you know what you're talking about, and they would feel comfortable trusting their clothing to your capable hands.

Almost any kind of business has a story idea in it. Heating oil and gas entrepreneurs could write about saving energy or keeping furnaces running properly. Hairdressers could write about caring for color-treated or permed hair, or for summer readers, minimizing sun damage at the beach. The possibilities are endless!

News Events

You can get free publicity by having a reporter write an article for you.

To do this, you need to create a situation that would be interesting to the local press. In publicity circles, this is called creating news.

Community service makes great news and has the added benefit of making you look benevolent. Sponsor a fundraising dinner for a local volunteer organization. Organize a marathon to benefit a health organization. Give your employees a few hours off each month to care for the homeless.

If community service doesn't appeal to you, try doing something outrageous. Get a tightrope walker to put on a show in front of your store. Start a controversy by taking an unusual stand on issues of importance in your community.

4. Publicity
   — Feature Articles
   — News Events
   — Presentations and Lectures

There's always something that begs doing. If you're the one to do it, you can attract the attention of reporters in your area.

Presentations and Lectures

Another way to get publicity, used successfully by a wide variety of business people, is to give lectures and classes to groups in your area. If you're a bicycle retailer, you could teach an adult education course on basic bike maintenance. Real estate agents could teach about first-time home buying. Travel agents could give lectures on international currency exchange and unusual vacations.

You could also make presentations to amateur and professional groups in your area. If you are in retail clothing, you might give a workshop on "The Look of Success" to local chapters of executive or business organizations. Child care entrepreneurs could talk about after-school care to a chapter of the local PTA. The possibilities are endless, and they eventually add up to money in the bank for you.

The End Result

You probably have generated a number of ideas for promoting your business while reading this chapter. Take a minute to jot these down. Your next step is to show your ideas to a professional who can advise you on the best combination of advertising and promotion for your needs. Then get ready to see your business's name in lights!

Building Your Public Image
Step by Step

1. **What Image Do You Want Your Business to Have?**
    Make Your Decision Based On:
    — The Type of Business You Have
    — Your Target Area
    — Your Target Customers

2. **Once You've Decided. . .**
    — Be Consistent
    — Promote, Promote, Promote

3. **Advertising Options**
    — Newspapers, Magazines, etc.
    — Television, Radio
    — Direct Mail
    — Display Ads
    — Classified Ads
    — Business Cards, Printed Pencils, Cups,
      T-shirts, etc.
    — Catalogues, Brochures
    — Telemarketing
    — Signs, Posters, Billboards
    — Yellow Pages and Other Directories

4. **Publicity**
    — Feature Articles
    — News Events
    — Presentations and Lectures

Your Road Map To Success
"i can." ™

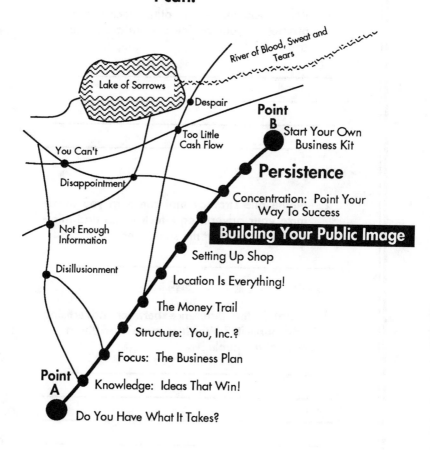

Chapter Checkpoint

1. Before you make any other decisions about promoting your business what must you decide first?

   _____

   _____

   _____

   _____

2. Name one strategy that can help you maximize your advertising effectiveness and minimize your costs at the same time.

   _____

3. What is the difference between advertising and publicity? Which is more credible in the eyes of the public?

   _____

   _____

   _____

   _____

   _____

_____

_____

_____

_____

_____

4. There are two basic ways you can attract
    publicity to yourself and your business. What
    are they?

_____

_____

Notes

9

Point Your Way to Success

"Success is relative. It is what we can make of the mess we have made of things."

— T. S. Eliot

Notes

Point Your Way To Success

You Can Start Your Own Business, like the other books in the "i can."™ series, is like a road sign that points your way to success. At this juncture in your reading, you have gained the benefit of years of business experience, saving yourself from having to learn what works — and what doesn't — on your own.

Your Road Map To Success
"i can." ™

Before we say farewell, let's go over some of the ground we've covered.

In Chapter One, **Do You Have What It Takes?**, we looked at what it means to be an entrepreneur and the kinds of qualities often found in successful business owners. It takes drive, adaptability, energy, determination and an abiding commitment to what you are doing.

Chapter Two, **Ideas that Win!**, discussed ideas — the foundation and starting point of any business. Not only should your idea be practical and affordable, it also must have the potential to fill a need. And, you have to like your idea. Without enthusiasm, you will lack sufficient energy for turning your idea into reality.

Chapter Three, **The Business Plan — Mapping Your Road to Success**, gave you information on how to take a vital first step — putting together your business plan. In this chapter, we outlined the business of starting a business.

The thrust of Chapter Four, **You, Inc.?**, was legal definition of the three main forms of ownership in business. In the sole proprietorship, you are the boss — and solely responsible for the company's assets, liabilities and capital. We discussed the partnership, where responsibility for the business is shared by two or more people. Finally, there is the corporation, a legal entity in which assets, liabilities and capital are independent, keeping business and private obligations separate.

How to get the money to start your business was the subject of Chapter Five, **The Money Trail**. Whether you plan to finance your start-up through family savings, bank loans, venture-capitalist funds or the government, you can get the most mileage on the money trail by following the advice in Chapter Five.

Chapter Six, **Location Is Everything!**, discussed where you should set up your business. It showed what to look for in terms of competition, traffic patterns, and other factors when choosing a site.

Chapter Seven, **Setting Up Shop**, concerned rents and leases, furniture and equipment and the all-important task of keeping the books.

Suppose you have the right personality, a winning idea, a good business plan, all the money you need, a perfect location and a fool-proof bookkeeping system. What more could you possibly need?

Customers, for one. Chapter Eight, **Building Your Public Image**, was devoted to helping you spread the word about your business to the people who count: potential customers. It discussed the difference between publicity and advertising, and gave a rundown of the avenues you can take to bring customers to your door.

Beginning the Journey

Now you're educated. The rest is up to you. You need to do more than reading and thinking and planning. You need to start doing.

Starting and running a business is not so much having something as doing something. It's not so much getting as getting things done. Starting a business is like starting a journey. Once you've committed yourself, you find that the journey has already begun. *Bon Voyage!*

Your Road Map To Success
"i can." ™

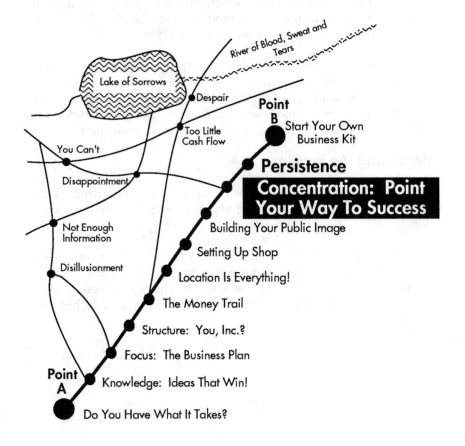

Notes

Notes

The Start Your Own Business Kit

1) Articles of Incorporation
2) Corporation Bylaws
3) Agreement to Form a Business Corporation
4) Subchapter S Resolution and Consent to Election
5) Partnership Agreement

— Articles of Incorporation —

ARTICLES OF INCORPORATION
OF
EVERYMAN'S CORPORATION, INC.

We, the undersigned, natural persons of full age, do make and acknowledge the Articles of Incorporation for the purpose of forming a business corporation under, and by virtue of the State of _____.

ARTICLE I
The name of the corporation shall be Everyman's Corporation, Inc.

ARTICLE II
The period of duration of the corporation shall be unlimited.

ARTICLE III
The purposes for which the Corporation is organized are:
(1) to engage in the business of _____, and, (2) to engage into any other lawful activity, including, but not limited to, sales, construction, manufacturing, raising or otherwise producing, and servicing, storing or otherwise caring for any type of structure, commodity, or livestock whatsoever; processing, selling, brokering, factoring, distributing, lending, borrowing or investing in any type of property whether real or personal, tangible or intangible; extracting and processing natural resources; transporting freight or passengers by land, sea, or air; collecting and disseminating information or advertisement through any medium whatsoever; performing in any type of management, investigative, advisory, promotional, protective, insurance, guarantyship, suretyship, fiduciary or representative capacity or relationship for any persons or corporations whatsoever.

ARTICLE IV
The Corporation shall have authority to issue _____ shares of common stock of par value of $___ per share.

ARTICLE V
The minimum amount of consideration to be received by the Corporation if its shares before it shall commence business is $_____ in cash or property of equivalent value.

ARTICLE VI
The address of the registered corporation is 100 Main Street, Anytown, Anystate 12345 and the name of the initial registered agent at such address is _____.

ARTICLE VII
The number of directors constituting the initial Board of Directors shall be _____ (__) and the names and addresses of the persons who shall serve as Directors until the first meeting of the shareholders, or until their successors are elected and qualified, are:

<u>NAME:</u>   <u>ADDRESS:</u>

Director 1   123 Anystreet
                  Anytown, Anystate 12345

Director 2   123 Anystreet
                  Anytown, Anystate 12345

The name and address of the Incorporator is:
<u>NAME:</u>   <u>ADDRESS:</u>

Incorporator   123 Anystreet
                  Anytown, Anystate 12345

IN WITNESS WHEREOF, I have hereunto set my hand, this the _____ day of _____ (month), 19___.

_____

Incorporator

I, the undersigned Notary Public in and for the said county and state, do hereby certify that _____ personally appeared before me this day and acknowledged the due execution of the fore-going instrument.

WITNESS my hand and Notarial Seal, this _____day of _____(month), 19___.

_____
Notary Public

My Commission Expires: _____ (date)

— Corporation Bylaws —

BYLAWS
FOR
EVERYMAN'S CORPORATION, INC.

ARTICLE I

The name of this corporation shall be _____. Its principal office shall be located at _____ in the City of _____, State of _____. Other offices for the transaction of business shall be located at such other places as the Board of Directors may from time to time determine.

ARTICLE II

The total authorized capital stock of this corporation shall be _____ shares of common stock of: (check applicable line):
__ a. No par.
__ b. Par value of $_____.
__ c. Preferred stock, as   follows:

_____.

All certificates of stock shall be signed by the President and the Secretary and shall be sealed with the corporate seal.

Treasury stock shall be held by the corporation subject to the disposal of the Board of Directors, and shall neither vote nor participate in dividends.

The corporation shall have a first lien on all the shares of its capital stock, and upon all dividends declared upon the same, for any indebtedness of the respective holders thereof to the corporation.

Transfers of stock shall be made only on the books of the corporation; and the old certificate, properly endorsed, shall be surrendered and cancelled before a new certificate is issued.

In case of loss or destruction of a certificate of stock, no new certificate shall be issued in lieu thereof except upon satisfactory proof to the Board of Directors of such loss or destruction; and upon the giving of satisfactory security against loss to the corporation; any such certificate shall be plainly marked "Duplicate" upon its face.

ARTICLE III
An annual meeting of the stockholders shall be held at _____ o'clock on the _____(day) of _____ (month) each year, commencing on the _____(day) of _____ (month) 19__, or if said date shall be a holiday, on the following day, at the principal office of the corporation. At such meeting the stockholders shall elect directors to serve until their successors are elected and qualified.

A special meeting of the stockholders, to be held at the same place as the annual meeting, may be called at any time whenever requested by stockholders holding a majority of the outstanding stock.

Unless prohibited by law, the stockholders holding a majority of the outstanding shares entitled to vote may, at any time, terminate the term of office of all or any of the directors, with or without cause, by a vote at any annual or special meeting, or by written statements, signed by the holders of a majority of such stock, and filed with the secretary or, in his absence, with any other officer. Such removal shall be effective immediately even if successors are not elected simultaneously, and the vacancies on the board of directors shall be filled only by the stockholders.

Notice of the time and place of all annual and special meetings shall be given 10 days before the date thereof, except that notice may be waived on consent of stockholders owning the following proportion of the outstanding stock (Check applicable line):
 __ a. A majority.
 __ b. Two-thirds majority.
 __ c. Three-fourths majority.
 __ d. Other _____.

The President, or in his absence, the Vice-President, shall preside at all meetings of the stockholders.

At every such meeting, each stockholder of common stock shall be entitled to cast one vote for each share of stock held in his name, which vote may be cast by him either in person, or by proxy. All proxies shall be in writing, and shall be filed with the Secretary and by him entered of record in the minutes of the meeting.

ARTICLE IV
The business and property of the corporation shall be managed by a board of not less than three or by an executive committee appointed by said board.

The regular meeting of the directors shall be held immediately after the adjournment of each annual stockholders' meeting. Special meetings of the board of directors may be called by the President.

Notice of all regular and special meetings shall be mailed to each director, by the Secretary, at least 10 days before such meeting, unless such notice is waived.

A quorum for the transaction of business at any meeting of the directors shall consist of a majority of the members of the board.

The directors shall elect the officers of the corporation and fix their salaries. Such election shall be held at the directors' meeting following each annual stockholders' meeting. Any officer may be removed, with or without cause, by vote of the directors at any regular or special meeting, unless such removal is prohibited by law.

Vacancies in the board of directors may be filled by the remaining directors at any regular or special meeting of the directors, except when such vacancy shall occur through removal by stockholders holding a majority of the outstanding shares, as hereinabove provided.

At each annual stockholders' meeting, the directors shall submit a statement of the business done during the preceding year, together with a report of the general financial condition of the corporation, and of the condition of its property.

ARTICLE V

The officers of the corporation shall be a President, a Vice-President, a Secretary, and a Treasurer (and, in the discretion of the directors, an assistant secretary), who shall be elected for a term of one year, and shall hold office until their successors are elected and qualified.

The President shall preside at all directors' and stockholders' meetings; shall sign all stock certificates and written contracts and undertakings of the corporation; and shall perform all such other duties as are incident to his office. In case of disability or absence from the city of the President, his duties shall be performed by the Vice-President, who shall have equal and concurrent powers.

The Secretary shall issue notice of all directors' and stockholders' meetings; shall attend and keep the minutes of such meetings; and shall perform all such other duties as are incident to his office. In case of disability or absence, his duties shall be performed by the assistant secretary, if any.

The Treasurer shall have custody of all money and securities of the corporation. He shall keep regular books of account and shall submit them, together with all his vouchers, receipts, records, and other papers, to the directors for their examination and approval as often as they may require; and shall perform all such duties as are incident to his office.

ARTICLE VI

Dividends, to be paid out of the surplus earnings of the corporation, may be declared from time to time by resolution of the board of directors by vote of a majority thereof.

The funds of the corporation shall be deposited in such bank or banks as the directors shall designate, and shall be withdrawn only upon the check of the corporation, signed as the directors shall from time to time resolve.

ARTICLE VII
Amendments to these Bylaws may be made by a vote of the stockholders holding a majority of the outstanding stock at any annual or special meeting, the notice of such special meeting to contain the nature of the proposed amendment.

We hereby adopt and ratify the foregoing Bylaws:

_____   _____
DIRECTOR   DATE

_____   _____
DIRECTOR   DATE

_____   _____
DIRECTOR   DATE

_____   _____
DIRECTOR   DATE

— Agreement to Form a Business Corporation —

AGREEMENT

AGREEMENT made the _____ (day) of _____ (month), 19__, between _____ (Incorporator 1), doing business under the trade name _____ (name of Incorporator 1's business) (herein called "Inc. 1"), and _____ (Incorporator 2), (herein called "Inc. 2").

Whereas, Inc. 1 and Inc. 2 have agreed to organize a corporation to which Inc. 1 will assign and transfer his _____ business, and in which Inc. 2 will subscribe for shares in an amount equal to the net worth of Inc. 1's business, on the following terms:

IT IS AGREED:

I.   **Formation of corporation.** Inc. 1 and Inc. 2 shall organize a corporation under the laws of the state of _____ to be known as _____ (name of the new business) (hereinafter called the "Corporation"), which shall begin business on the ___ (day) of _____ (month), 19__.

II. **Certificate of incorporation.** The Corporation shall be organized so as to provide for the following:

(a) The duration of the Corporation shall be perpetual.
(b) The number of directors shall be two.
(c) The aggregate number of shares that the Corporation shall have authority to issue shall be _____ shares _____ (with/ without) par value common stock (par value equal to _____).
(d) The Purposes of the Corporation shall include the _____, and all other purposes necessary for the continued and expanded operation of the business now conducted by Inc. 1 and the development of new business.

(e) The principal place of business of the corporation shall be in the County of _____, and State of _____.

(f)   A copy of the proposed Articles of Incorporation is attached hereto as Exhibit A.

III. Distribution of shares. Upon incorporation, the shares of the Corporation shall be issued as follows:

(a) To Inc. 1: Fifty (50) common no-par shares, fully paid and nonassessable, for which Inc. 1 shall transfer to the Corporation, on ___ (day) of _____ (month), 19__, all the assets of his business, subject to all its liabilities. Upon such transfer, the Corporation shall assume all such liabilities. No other consideration shall be paid to _____ for such transfer, and he shall accept the 50 common no-par shares in full payment.

(b) To Inc. 2: 50 common no-par shares, fully paid and nonassessable, for which Inc. 2 shall pay to the Corporation, on ___ (day) of _____ (month), 19__, an amount in cash equivalent to the net worth of the assets transferred by Inc. 1 to the Corporation, as shown by a balance sheet to be prepared by _____, certified public accounts. In the preparation of this balance sheet, the value of all assets shall be taken as shown on the books of _____ on ___ (day) of _____ (month), 19__, and all liabilities shall be similarly taken, except that no liability of _____for income taxes shall be recorded on the books of the Corporation. No other consideration shall be paid to Inc. 2 for such payment, and he shall accept the 50 common no-par shares in full satisfaction of the payment so made to the Corporation.

IV. Control. Inc. 1 and Inc. 2 shall vote their shares whenever appropriate so as to provide for the following:

(a) The directors shall be: Inc. 1 and Inc. 2.

(b) The officers shall be: President: Inc. 1; Secretary & Treasurer: Inc. 2.

(c) All corporate checks shall be signed by the President and countersigned by the Treasurer.

(d) Inc. 1 shall be employed by the Corporation as general manager at an annual salary of $_____, payable in equal semimonthly installments. _____ shall devote his entire time and efforts to the affairs of the Corporation. Such employment and compensation shall end, however, upon the death or disability of _____. No other compensation shall be paid to _____ for services rendered as an officer or director of the Corporation.

(e) Inc. 2 shall be employed by the Corporation as sales manager at an annual salary of $_____, payable in equal semimonthly installments. Inc. 2 shall devote his entire time and efforts to the affairs of the Corporation. Such employment and compensation shall end, however, upon the death or disability of Inc. 1. No other compensation shall be paid to Inc. 2 for services rendered as an officer or director of the Corporation.

V. Representations. To induce Inc. 2 to enter into this Agreement, Inc. 1 represents the following:

(a) He is not a party to any litigation, nor is the business now operated by him involved in any legal controversy that could reasonably be foreseen to lead to litigation.

(b) The books of the business do not reflect any values for goodwill, trade names, trademarks, patents, or any similar intangibles.

(c) The various trade names and labels for plants and products now in use by him have been used in the past without interference or adverse claim, and all ownership that he may have in these trade names and labels shall be included in the proposed transfer to the Corporation together with all other intangible assets of the business.

(d) Until transferred to the Corporation, the business shall be operated only in the manner heretofore conducted. No purchase or disbursement shall be made and no expense or liability shall be incurred except in accordance with prior practice.

(e) He has procured the consent of the landlord to the assignment of the lease covering the premises now occupied by his business in _____ (town), _____ (county), _____ (state).

(f) He will warrant and defend the title of all assets transferred by him to the Corporation against all claims and all persons, except as to the liabilities as shown on the balance sheet to be prepared by _____ (accountants).

VI. **Legal Services.** All legal services required in connection with the organization of the Corporation and with performance of the various provisions of this agreement shall be performed by _____ (lawyer), and his charge for such services, plus all necessary disbursements incurred by him in the performance of the services, shall be paid by the Corporation.

VII. **Implementation of this agreement.** Inc. 1 and Inc. 2 shall promptly execute all documents required to carry out the terms of this Agreement.

IN WITNESS WHEREOF, I have hereunto set my hand, this the _____ day of _____ (month), 19___.

_____   _____
Incorporator 1   Date

_____   _____
Incorporator 2   Date

I, the undersigned Notary Public in and for the said county and state, do hereby certify that _____ and _____ personally appeared before me this day and acknowledged the due execution of the foregoing instrument.

WITNESS my hand and Notarial Seal, this _____day of _____(month), 19___.

_____
Notary Public

My Commission Expires: _____ (date)

—Subchapter S Resolution—

SUBCHAPTER S CORPORATION
RESOLUTION

Resolved, that the Treasurer of this Corporation be and is hereby author-ized to take any and all action necessary to comply with the requirements of the Internal Revenue Service for making an election pursuant to Subchapter S of the Internal Revenue Code, Section 1372.

CONSENT TO ELECTION
AS SUBCHAPTER S CORPORATION

In accordance with the provisions of Section 1372, Internal Revenue Code, and the regulations issued thereunder, the undersigned, all the share-holders of _____ (name of corporation), a corporation formed under the laws of the state of _____ (name of state), do hereby consent to the election made by that Corporation on Treasury Department Form 2553 to which this Statement is attached, and do hereby submit the following information:

(a) The name and address of the Corporation is:

Name
123 Anystreet, Anytown, Anystate, 12345

(b) The name and address of each shareholder of the Corporation, the number of shares of stock owned by him, and the date or dates on which such stock was acquired, are as follows:

NAME	ADDRESS	SHARES	DATE
Shareholder 1	123 Anystreet Anytown, Anystate 12345	000	Date
Shareholder 2	123 Anystreet Anytown, Anystate 12345	000	Date
Shareholder 3	123 Anystreet Anytown, Anystate 12345	000	Date

_____   _____
Shareholder 1   Date

                                                    _____   _____
                                                    Shareholder 3   Date

_____   _____
Shareholder 2   Date

— Partnership Agreement —

PARTNERSHIP AGREEMENT

AGREEMENT, made in _____ (city), _____ (state), on the _____ (day) of _____ (month), 19__, between _____ (Partner 1), residing at _____ (address), and _____ (Partner 2), residing at _____ (address),

WHEREAS, the parties hereto desire to form a partnership for the purpose of _____; and WHEREAS, the Partners have stipulated their mutual rights, powers, duties, and liabilities in connection with the business of the partnership;

NOW THEREFORE, in consideration of the mutual covenants given herein, the Partners agree as follows:

I. **Name.** The name of the partnership shall presently be _____, or such other name as the Partners may later agree upon.

II. **Purpose.** The purposes of the partnership shall be to _____, and to do anything necessary or incidental to the foregoing.

III. **Office.** The principal office of the partnership shall be located at _____, or at such other place as the Partners may agree.

IV. **Term.** The provisions of this Agreement shall become binding upon all of the Partners at the time this Agreement is signed by all of the Partners, and said partnership shall continue indefinitely unless terminated by mutual agreement of the Partners, or as may hereinafter be provided.

V. **Management.** No Partner may do any act on behalf of the partnership without the consent of the other Partners, which act is not within the scope of the purposes of the partnership as set forth in Paragraph II above. Any partnership decision having a substantial effect upon the interest of the partnership, or of any Partner, shall require the unanimous agreement of the Partners. Provided however, it is expressly agreed that _____ (executor's name) may execute any and all documents, and the signature of _____ (executor's name) to any such document shall bind the partnership.

VI. Capital Contributions.

A. The Partners shall make initial capital contributions in the following amounts:

Partner 1	$000,000.00
Partner 2	$000,000.00

B. The profits and losses of the partnership and distributions of the partnership, including distributions to Partners upon the dissolution of the partnership, shall be allocated to the partners according to the following percentages:

Partner 1	00%
Partner 2	00%

VII. **Additional Capital.** It is recognized by the Partners that capital, in addition to the initial contributions set forth above, may be required by the partnership to accomplish the purposes of the partnership. In such event, the Partners shall make additional contributions or loans to the partnership, and such contributions or loans shall be made in proportion to the ownership of the Partners as set forth in Paragraph VI above.

VIII. **Other Activities of Partners.** It is acknowledged that each of the Partners has other interest in business, and shall be permitted to continue their other business activities notwithstanding their status as Partners, nor shall any of them be required to devote their full time to the partnership's business, but only such part as may be necessary to reasonably develop and manage it.

IX. **Banking.** All funds of the partnership shall be deposited in its name in such checking account or accounts in such bank or banks as agreed upon by the Partners. All withdrawals therefrom are to be made upon checks signed by any Partner or by such person as may be designated by the Partners.

X. **Books.** The books of the partnership shall be maintained at its principal office, in accordance with generally accepted accounting principles, and any Partner or his representative shall have access thereto during all reasonable business hours. The fiscal year of the partnership shall end on December 31st in each year or on such other date as the Partners shall determine, and the books shall be closed and balanced at the end of each year. Statements showing the receipts and disbursements in each calendar month shall be prepared and distributed to the Partners at least quarterly. Periodic balance sheets shall be furnished as often as deemed necessary by the Partners.

XI. **Compensation.** No compensation, salaries, fees, or commissions shall be paid by the partnership to any Partner herein for any services rendered to the partnership, except as expressly agreed to, from time to time, by the Partners.

XII. **Sale of Partnership Interest.**
A. Any Partner may assign all or portions of his interest in the partnership to another Partner or to his spouse, children, parents, or to a trust created for the benefit of the foregoing. In the event of such assignment, the assignee shall not be admitted as a Partner, but shall have an interest only in the profits of the partnership as in existence on the date hereof.
B. Except, as set forth in Subparagraph A above, no Partner may sell, assign, transfer, or otherwise dispose of his interest in this partnership without the written consent of the other Partners herein, except as follows:

(a) A Partner may sell part or all of his interest in this partnership to any third party provided he shall:
  (i) First offer such interest to the other Partners herein
       at the same price and on the same terms as to the
       third party, whose identity must be stated in the
       offer; and
  (ii) If such offer is not accepted by the other Partners in
       the partnership within fifteen (15) days from the
       date of such offer, the offerer may sell to the desig-
       nated third party at the price and terms specified
       within ninety (90) days after the expiration of the
       said 15-day period.
  (iii) Thereafter, before any contemplated sale, the
       interest must again be offered to the other Partners.
  (iv) Nothing herein shall imply that the Partners may
       purchase less than all of the interest being offered.
(b) Any Partner may sell all or part of his interest to the other
Partners.
(c) Any such sale, transfer, assignment, or other disposition,
however, shall not have any operative force or effect
unless:
  (i) The instrument of transfer provides that the assignee
       shall be bound by all of the terms and conditions of
       this Agreement as if the assignee were a party who
       had joined in the execution and delivery hereof; and
  (ii) A duplicate original of the instrument of transfer is
       delivered to this partnership and to all the Partners
       herein.

XIII. Death of a Partner.

A. In the event of the death of a Partner, the partnership shall not
be dissolved. The legal representative of the deceased Partner
shall, within seven (7) days of the death of the Partner, elect
either to retain the partnership interest of the deceased Partner,
or to sell such interest to the surviving Partners upon the terms
and conditions set forth below. Failure of the legal representative of the deceased Partner to make an election pursuant to

this paragraph shall be deemed to be an election by said legal representative to retain the partnership interest. In the event the interest of the deceased Partner is retained, the owner of such interest shall not be admitted as a Partner, but shall have an interest only in the profits of the partnership. In the event the legal representative of the deceased elects to sell the interest to the partnership, the purchase price of such interest shall be the sum of:

(a) Credits to the decedent on the partnership's books for loans made to the partnership;

(b) Undisturbed profits to the date of death;

(c) The value of the deceased Partner's interest in the partnership and its assets, including his capital account as of the date of death, but exclusive of the amount of preceding items (a) and (b).

Interest shall accrue on such amount at ____Percent (__%) per annum from the date of death and shall be paid quarter-annually and without regard to the earnings of the partnership. Items (i) and (ii) shall be determined by the certified public accountants retained by the partnership by reference to the books of account.

B. If the parties to the sale cannot agree upon the value of item (c) within fifteen (15) days after the determination of the preceding items (a) and (b) by the said certified public accountants, then the value thereof shall be determined by appraisal in the following manner:

(a) Within seven (7) days after the expiration of the aforementioned fifteen (15) day period, one appraiser shall be selected by the surviving Partners and one appraiser shall be selected by the representative of the deceased partner, and written notice thereof shall be given to the other parties, and said two appraisers determination as to value shall be conclusive and binding.

(b) In the event either party fails or refuses to select an appraiser and give notice thereof within the seven (7) day period mentioned in preceding Subparagraph (a), the determination of value made by the appraiser selected by the other party shall be conclusive and binding upon the parties.

(c) If two appraisers are selected in the foregoing manner but cannot agree on a determination of value within fifteen (15) days after the expiration of the seven (7) day period mentioned in Subparagraph A, then said two appraisers shall select a third appraiser, whose determination of value shall be conclusive and binding upon both parties.

(d) If the said two appraisers cannot agree upon a third appraiser within ten (10) days after the expiration of the fifteen (15) day period mentioned in the preceding (c), then such third appraiser shall be appointed by the Presiding Judge of _____ (county, state), upon petition of either party.

(e) The cost of such appraisal shall be shared equally by the parties.

C. The purchase price determined hereunder shall be payable in no more than ten equal annual installments, the first to be made within thirty (30) days after the determination of the purchase price. The purchase price may be prepaid at any time without penalty.

XIV. **Bankruptcy.** If any of the Partners shall be adjudicated bankrupt or insolvent pursuant to the provisions of any state or federal insolvency or bankruptcy act, or if a receiver or trustee shall be appointed for all or a portion of such Partner's property, or if any execution or other process Partner's property shall be made for the benefit of creditors, or if any execution or other process shall issue against any Partner's interest in the partnership, and if not vacated within ninety (90) days (hereinafter under any of the foregoing circumstances called the "Attached Partner") then and in any such event, the other Partners shall have the right and option to acquire all the Attached Partner's interest in the partnership at a price equivalent to the Attached Partner's capital contribution and loans, if any, to the partnership, less any cash distributions previously made by the partnership to the Attached Partner and less any repayments of loans. Such right and option shall be exercisable in writing within thirty (30) days after such adjudication or order appointing receiver or trustee becomes final, or after such assignment for the benefit of creditors has been effected, or after the expiration of such ninety (90) day period following the issuance of any execution or other process against the Attached Partner's interest in the partnership, and the Attached Partner shall execute and deliver to the other party such deeds, assignments, and other documents as shall be necessary to convey all of his right, title, and interest in the partnership in proper and due form of transfer with all requisite transfer stamps affixed, free and clear of all encumbrances except such encumbrances to which the partnership shall have suffered as against payment of the purchase price. The Partners are hereby granted the irrevocable power of attorney to execute and deliver on behalf of the Attached Partner all such instruments.

XV. Failure of Partner to Make Additional Required Advances. In the event that one of the Partners shall fail to make an advance to the partnership required of him under this Agreement, and such default shall continue for a period of thirty (30) days after a call for such advance, then the other Partners shall have the following options:

A. To arrange for a loan to the partnership with interest of such defaulting Partner in the partnership, the amount of such loan and the interest thereon to be payable on demand by the defaulting Partner, and any distributions from the partnership otherwise payable to the defaulting Partner being first available for application against the aforesaid indebtedness; or

B. To purchase, within sixty (60) days after such default, the total interest of the defaulting Partner for the amount of said defaulting Partner's total contribution to the capital of the partnership and loans to the partnership, less any previous cash distributions made by the partnership to the defaulting Partner; or,

C. To make good such deficiency on the part of the defaulting Partner and then to reallocate the interest in the partnership of the defaulting Partner in the capital and profits of the partnership so that such defaulting partner's participation in the partnership and its profits and losses and his percentage of the cash flow therefrom shall be reduced to reflect his failure to make the aforesaid advances, and the interest in the partnership and in the profits thereof and the percentage of the cash flow there from of the Partner making good such deficiency shall be increased to reflect such advances in excess of his original obligation hereunder, and shall thereafter remain fixed as of the date of such default; or

D. To dissolve and terminate the partnership and have its assets liquidated and distributed, in which event the proceeds of such liquidation shall be distributed to the nondefaulting Partner to the full extent of his capital contributions plus any loans made by him to the partnership, before any distributions shall be made to the defaulting Partner.

XVI. **Notices.** Any notices and demands hereunder shall be in writing and shall be deemed to have been given and received forty-eight (48) hours after the same shall have been deposited in United States registered or certified mail, postage prepaid, to the following addresses:

> Partner 1   123 Anystreet
>   Anytown, Anystate 12345
>
> Partner 2   123 Anystreet
>   Anytown, Anystate 12345

Any Partner may change his address as set forth above by giving notice to the other Partners.

XVII. **Modification and Amendments.** No modifications or amendments to this partnership Agreement shall be valid or binding unless and until each such modification or amendment shall have been reduced to writing and executed by each of the parties hereto.

XVIII. **Successors.** This Agreement shall be binding upon the parties hereto and upon their heirs, successors, and assigns.

IN WITNESS WHEREOF, We have hereunto set our hands, this the _____ day of _____ (month), 19___.

_____   _____
Partner 1   Date

_____   _____
Partner 2   Date

I, the undersigned Notary Public in and for the said county and state, do hereby certify that _____ personally appeared before me this day and acknowledged the due execution of the foregoing instrument.

WITNESS my hand and Notarial Seal, this _____day of _____(month), 19___.

_____
Notary Public

My Commission Expires: _____ (date)

Notes

Further Reading

"Do you know the difference between education and experience? Education is when you read the fine print; experience is what you get when you don't."

— *Pete Seeger*

Bill Adler's Chance of a Lifetime. Bill Adler. New York: Warner, 1985.
This book covers every aspect of business start-up, from
determining what makes a successful business owner to
market research, getting loans, and keeping the books. Well-
organized, lively, and formatted for quick reference.

The Challenge. Robert Allen. New York: Simon and Schuster, 1987.
This is the true account of three people, unemployed and
undirected, who were guided by the author to become financial successes in 90 days. Throughout the book, Allen gives
"wealth secrets" that can make anyone financially successful
in practically no time, regardless of their current financial
status.

The Work-at-Home Sourcebook. Lynie Arden. Boulder: Live Oak,
1987.
Sourcebook lists the names and addresses of more than 1,000
companies that let you work independently and out of your
own home. Provides good practice for those who need to get
their feet wet in the ways of being self-employed.

Take a Chance to Be First:The Secrets of Entrepreneurial Success. Warren
Avis. New York: Macmillian, 1986.
The founder of Avis Rent-a-Car shares his hard-won wisdom
on what it takes to succeed in being your own boss. Well-
written and direct, the book inspires, informs, instructs and
entertains.

Getting to Yes: Negotiating Agreement Without Giving In. Roger Fisher
and William Ury. New York: Penguin, 1981.
Methods, tactics and strategies for coming to mutual agreements without getting the short end of the stick. Enormously
useful, since good negotiations are crucial to business success.

*Nobody Gets Rich Working for Somebody Else — An Entrepreneur's
Guide.* Roger Fritz. New York: Dodd, Mead, 1987.
This hands-on guide helps you make the right business
choices. It helps you to start on the right track and stay there.

How to Start and Manage Your Own Business. Gardner Greene. New
York: Bantam, 1975.
Written with the small businessperson in mind, this book
covers all aspects of starting and maintaining a business,
including selecting professional services, developing and
marketing products, negotiating, and working with the
government.

The Entrepreneur's Guide to Starting a Successful Business. James Halloran, Blue Ridge Summit, Pa.: Tab, 1987.
A serious and in-depth look at business start-up basics — business plans, market research and cash-flow operations, to name a few. Practical and direct, the book is packed with graphs, charts, diagrams, tables and illustrations.

Growing a Business. Paul Hawken. New York: Simon and Schuster, 1987.
In this companion volume to the popular PBS series, Hawken emphasizes the proper attitude you need to make your business grow. The purpose of business, he says, "is not to take risks, but to get things done."

How to Start Your Business on a Shoestring and Make up to $500,000 Per Year. Taylor Hicks. Rocklin, Ca.: Prima, 1987.
Chock-full of information, this book presents step-by-step techniques and procedures for starting a business at home. Included is a comprehensive list of more than 1,000 businesses you can start at home with little or no money down.

Think and Grow Rich. Napoleon Hill. New York: Fawcett, 1960.
One of the original what-to-do-and-how-to-do-it books. Napoleon Hill, writer of Franklin D. Roosevelt's "Nothing to Fear But Fear Itself" speech, pioneered the whole self-help field. Enormously influential and highly recommended.

The Entrepreneur's Guide: How to Start and Succeed in Your Own Business. Phillip Holland. New York: Putnam, 1984.
Self-made millionaire and founder of America's largest privately owned doughnut-shop franchise, Holland provides useful advice on all angles of business start-up, with an emphasis on retail. All it takes to start a business, according to Holland, is "guts, brains and capital."

Iacocca: An Autobiography. Lee Iacocca with William Novak. New York:Bantam, 1984.
A national best-seller by America's best-known CEO. Plentiful insights into the successful "corporate mind."

Entrepreneurism: the Mythical, the True, and the New. Thomas F. Jones with T. P. Elsaesser. New York: Fine, 1987.
The author calls this a "why-to" book. Drawing on conversations with successful entrepreneurs, as well as his own 20 years of business experience, Jones gets to the heart of what it really means to own a business and succeed.

101 Best Businesses to Start. Sharon Kahn and the Phillip Lief Group.
New York: Doubleday, 1988.
  Kahn and Co. give the 101 best businesses for the 1990s —
  each with a special section on how to start, initial investment
  and overhead, and time until financial break-even.

Lead, Follow, or Get Out of the Way: Leadership Strategies for the Thoroughly Modern Manager. James Lundy. San Diego: Avant, 1986.
  Easy-to-Read, entertaining, and effective, this book is for all
  those who are interested in improving performance and
  results through better communications and understanding.
  Includes useful tips on good leadership, the uses of power,
  goal-setting and getting things done.

Guts: Advertising from the Inside Out. John Lyons. New York: American Management Association, 1987.
  Gives you the straight dope from a real insider. Since promo-
  tion is crucial to business success, understanding advertising
  is invaluable when it comes to working with advertisers.

In Love and In Business: How Entrepreneurial Couples Are Changing the Rules of Business and Marriage. Sharon Nelton. New York:
Wiley, 1986.
  The author interviews 60 couples who successfully combine
  personal and business relationships. For couples considering
  going into business together, this is the book to read.

Fortune-Building Secrets of the Rich. Duane Newcomb. West Nyack,
N.Y.: Parker, 1983.
  How do people get rich and stay rich? This book tells all.
  Basically an "attitude" book, it reveals the formulas and tech-
  niques shared by those who have succeeded in their search
  for financial independence.

Do-It-Yourself Marketing Research. George Edward Sheen. New York:
McGraw-Hill, 1977.
  Intended for those with little or no experience in market
  research techniques and practices, this book offers practical
  advice and instructions for the entrepreneur who can't afford
  to hire a professional market research team. Highly useful
  and down-to-earth.

How to Avoid Lawyers: A Legal Guide for Layman. Edward Siegel. New
York: Fawcett, 1989.
  Lawyers are expensive. This book can be a real money-saver.
  The chapters on business start-up and knowing when to call
  in a lawyer are highly recommended.

Sweat Equity: What It Really Takes to Build America's Best Small Companies— By the Guys Who Did It. Geoffrey Smith and Paul Brown. New York: Simon and Schuster, 1986.

This book is about what to expect when you stop thinking and talking about starting your own business and actually try to make it happen. Compiled from interviews with the entrepreneurs who started today's fastest growing companies, the book is well-worth reading.

*Running Your Own Business: A Handbook of Facts and Information.*Howard Stern. New York: Crown, 1986.

Howard Stern calls his book "a primer for the businessman, especially the small businessman." It covers all aspects of operating a small business, and cuts through theory and background material to get right to the essentials.

Trump: The Art of the Deal. Donald Trump with Tony Schwartz. New York: Random House, 1987.

Trump on Trump. Takes you through a day, a week, and a life of one of America's most outspoken "movers and shakers." Includes Trump's own eleven guidelines for success, as well as his views on the art of the deal.

Notes

Index